Praise for Strategic Storytelling

"*This is an important book, one that you'll benefit from for years to come. Highly recommended.*"

Seth Godin, author of This is Marketing

"*This book will enable you to tell the right story, at the right time, to the right audience, to deliver the right outcome.*"

Paul Propster, Chief Story Architect, NASA/JPL STORY office

"*Through this book, Anjali helps leaders amplify their voices for bigger impact. This book is for everyone who wants to make their voices heard in the most compelling and authentic way. Anjali's approach to strategic storytelling not only magnifies meaning to each communication but also joins individual values to organizational mission, inspires trust, and connects dreams to reality. This book is also for those who may be worried that they will lose themselves in over-engineering or be over-strategic in their storytelling. Your readers will not lose their voices, but instead will find their voices.*"

Noom Poovarawan, ACC, Director at Airbnb, ex-Google,
ICF-Certified Coach, Fulbright Scholar

"*In this book Anjali has demystified storytelling in the corporate world.* Strategic Storytelling *makes a compelling case on why some stories drive your success at work and others don't. Very easy to read with use of simple vocabulary. Perfect for a busy corporate professional.*"

C. S. Chua, President and Managing Director at
Infineon Technologies

"*Before I met Anjali, I considered storytelling just as something casual and not something to be used in a corporate setting. I have now realized how* Strategic Storytelling *can be an extremely powerful tool for any leader in delivering their messages and capturing the heart and mind of their audience. This book encapsulates everything I have learned from Anjali, the master storyteller!*"

Pandai Othman, MD/CEO at Malaysia Marine & Heavy Engineering

T0271453

"Strategic Storytelling *is an excellent guide for anyone wanting to be successful in the corporate world. Anjali has done a masterful job of making stories relevant to the corporate professionals. I loved that the book doesn't just talk about the importance of storytelling but also has beautiful stories.*"

Cher Whee Sim, Vice President, Global Talent Acquisition, Mobility and Immigration at Micron Technology

"*The corporate world understood the power of storytelling some time ago. However, it is not just storytelling but strategic storytelling that sets you up for success. In this book, Anjali has shared brilliant lessons on making your stories strategic and impactful to your audience.*"

Grace Kerrison, Head of Sales Solutions—APAC at LinkedIn

"*This book is a must-read for anyone leading a meaningful change, whether in their organizations or their personal lives. I have seen transformative results from storytelling in my work with Anjali and I am delighted to now have this invaluable resource that simplifies and demystifies storytelling.*"

Rahil Hasan, Vice President, Learning, Development, and Wellbeing at Micron Technology

"*Having personally worked with Anjali on a large Digital Transformation Project back in 2016, I have firsthand experienced the power of storytelling in making a change happen in an organization. In her book,* Strategic Storytelling, *Anjali masterfully captures the storytelling insights that any corporate professional can use to drive their success*"

Laurent Filipozzi, General Manager at STMicroelectronics

Strategic Storytelling

Anjali Sharma

Strategic Storytelling

Why Some Stories Drive Your Success at
Work but Others Don't

Anjali Sharma

NICHOLAS BREALEY
PUBLISHING

London • Boston

First published by Nicholas Brealey Publishing in 2024
An imprint of John Murray Press
A division of Hodder & Stoughton Ltd,
An Hachette UK company

6

Illustrations by Ho Yin Mei

A CIP catalogue record for this title is available from the British Library

Trade Paperback ISBN 978 1 39980 4 738
eBook ISBN 978 1 39980 4 752

Typeset by KnowledgeWorks Global Ltd.

Printed and bound in Great Britain by Clays Ltd, Elcograf S.p.A.

John Murray Press policy is to use papers that are natural, renewable and recyclable products
and made from wood grown in sustainable forests. The logging and manufacturing processes
are expected to conform to the environmental regulations of the country of origin.

John Murray Press	Nicholas Brealey Publishing
Carmelite House	Hachette Book Group
50 Victoria Embankment	Market Place, Center 53, State Street
London EC4Y 0DZ	Boston, MA 02109, USA

www.nicholasbrealey.com

The authorised representative in the EEA is Hachette Ireland, 8 Castlecourt
Centre, Dublin 15, D15 XTP3, Ireland (email: info@hbgi.ie)

This book is dedicated to Ravi, my husband, for teaching me that you can't be a good storyteller unless you are willing to story-listen.

A special thank you to the following clients who gave me an opportunity to do some of my best work so far. Through that work came the many insights I shared in this book.

Rahil Hasan
C. S. Chua
Mohamad Firouz Asnan
Nazrin Banu Shaikh S. Ahmad
Pandai Othman
Cher Whee Sim
Grace Kerrison
Noom Poovarawan
Christina Marie Woodwick
Jane Grenier
Laurent Filipozzi
Gan Siok Hoon
Datuk Bacho Pilong
Wong Lin
Mahendar Nayak

And a special thanks to my colleague and friend, Benj, for all his support over the years.

Contents

(Estimated reading time in parenthesis)

Part III: How to Tell a Strategic Corporate Narrative

Preface

There are four dead bodies lying in a row.

What's happened? Not one, not two, but all four plant workers were dead. Had some evil supernatural power been at play? Some wondered.

No. The reason for the four deaths was as scientific as it can get.

It happened at a liquefied natural gas plant. It was a normal working day with 5,000 workers on-site wearing hard hats and bright-colored overalls. They were all busy catching up with their work.

In one corner of the plant site, a worker—let's call him Rahim—was welding a 60-inch pipe. To give you some perspective, a 60-inch pipe is so huge a human can walk into it. And then for whatever reason Rahim went inside the pipe.

Some suspected Rahim wanted to inspect the weld from inside. Nevertheless, no one thought too much about his decision to go inside the pipe. Each of them continued with their respective duties for the day.

After a while some of the coworkers noticed an unusual amount of time had passed. Rahim was still inside the pipe.

Concerned about the safety of his coworker, another worker went inside the pipe to have a look. Mind you, as per safety procedures, no one should go into a confined space like a pipe without a special permit and, in some cases, breathing equipment. But in the panic to work out what had happened to Rahim, he went in and never came out again.

By this time, a crowd had started to build on-site, and people were getting worried. In the worry, panic, and stress, a third worker went inside the pipe. Unfortunately, just like the other two workers, he didn't come out either.

A dear friend of one of the workers inside the pipe had heard what had happened and wanted to save his friend. In his eagerness to save his friend, he dashed toward the pipe. The crowd tried to stop him, but he was a large man who used his strength to push people aside. Sadly, he made his way through into the pipe.

And guess what? He too never came out! One after the other, they all never came out of the pipe that tragic day.

It was a crisis overtaken by panic and a complete lack of control, calm, and consensus among the bystanders on what was the right thing to do. What seemed like the most obvious thing to do was to go inside the pipe and help, but in this case the obvious was not the right thing to do.

Eventually, the site supervisor and staff with proper safety and breathing equipment went into the pipe. What they saw was beyond anyone's comprehension or imagination.

They saw four dead bodies lying in a row.

A normal process while welding a pipe is to flow inert gas onto the area being welded. This shields the weld from oxygen and water vapor to ensure the quality of the weld. Inert gas has no oxygen.

When the workers went inside, they inhaled inert gas without any oxygen, asphyxiated, and collapsed. If Rahim and the other workers had followed the safety protocol, they would have taken the breathing equipment with them, and events would have turned out drastically different.

The same evening the site construction manager did a postmortem of the incident—a big American guy nicknamed "Wild Bill." He was a true Texan cowboy who had a larger-than-life personality. He was choking on his tears as he addressed the workers.

Finally, he managed to clear his throat, summoning just enough strength to speak for a few seconds: "My job tonight is to knock on the door of this guy's house and tell his seven-year-old son his dad is not coming home. You don't want my job."

That day, I learned a lesson for life. If 5,000 workers come on-site, it's my job to make sure 5,000 people come off-site the same day. I don't want to lose a single person.

So, the safety of my team is the most important thing for me. As their leader, their friend, and the person entrusted by their family to take care of their safety. There are no compromises, no excuses, no cutting corners, no explanations, and no justifications when it comes to safety protocols. Safety comes first, always.

* * *

This story was told by a client of mine to his team members in 2014 as he stepped into his new role as plant head. Years later, this story remains one of the best stories I have helped my client find, curate, and tell to make a desired change happen. The desired change in this case was to ensure that the site workers didn't just say, "Safety comes first," but practiced it, too. This is a common challenge in high-risk working environments.

With my client's permission, I captured this story in a blog and shared it on my social channels. As expected, it garnered a lot of love. This story became so popular in the organization that in the subsequent years, while I was working with different departments of the same company, people would come and tell me the story they had read in a blog doing the rounds, unaware that the blog was authored by me. I smiled and enjoyed the popularity of the story.

My client leveraged the power of this story by telling it several times. The emotional gravitas of the story had the audience in tears every time. The audience could imagine their families suffering if they failed to follow the safety protocols in their high-risk working environments. And, most importantly, the emotion embedded in the story moved people into taking action.

My client's powerful storytelling not only made the desired change happen but also drove his own success in the organization. I often heard his name being touted as an inspirational leader in the company. This story, with its high pull factor, became a springboard to his success.

It's a remarkable story.

As Seth Godin has taught us, *remarkable* means something worthy of being remarked at. In the process of remarking we spread the story.

But are remarkable stories always the best stories for the corporate world?

The Danger of Remarkable Stories

The danger with this story lies in its remarkability. Yes, you read that right, the *danger*. After becoming aware of this story, it is natural for us to want to use it to make the point that "safety comes first." We want to replicate my client's success for ourselves. What we see and comprehend is success with this story for my client and we desire the same success. But hang on, there's more to storytelling than just telling a good story, in this case a remarkable story.

The reason my client was successful with his storytelling was not just because he had a remarkable story to tell. It was also because it was a *strategic* choice for the settings where he was telling it and because he had a deep understanding of *whom he was telling the story to.*

Let's explore whether this same remarkable story would always have the same impact, regardless of where or to whom it was told. Imagine you are responsible for the safety of a plant. The only way you can resolve an anticipated safety issue is by shutting the plant down for a week, upgrading the machinery, and at the same time running programs to make sure all the factory workers are aware of the safety protocols associated with the use of the newly installed gear. You strongly feel that an upgrade is required in terms of both machinery and staff knowledge. You go to your boss and tell this story to make a point—safety comes first. You confidently expect to be given permission to shut the plant for a week. But that doesn't happen: Most likely your boss will say, "Find another way. We can't shut the plant down." You walk out of that boardroom feeling defeated. You thought you had a great story, so why did you get this response?

At this stage, if you are thinking that the boss would never respond in that way, most likely, you have never worked in a plant. Keep reading, I will shortly respond to this thought surfacing in your mind.

Back to why did you get this response? It may have something to do with ...

Getting the Right Emotion to Build Connection

A human-centric story purely built on emotion isn't wrong, but it's not enough on its own to drive the change we want in corporate boardrooms. My point isn't that emotion has no role to play in such settings. The key here is not to strip the story of emotions, but to use these emotions to find the motivation, build resonance, create connection with the audience in question, and move people to take the right action.

If you read the last line, but didn't really connect with it, fret not, you are like most corporate professionals who are inundated with words like *motivation, resonance, connection,* and *action.* The overuse of these meaningful words has led to them being ignored. I promise, I will explain each of these shortly. They are not only meaningful but also important for your corporate success.

Back to Your Boss

Although your boss is human, they also have the responsibility of dealing with the practicalities of running the business. Businesses have to make profits, though, granted, not at the cost of human lives: They do have to do well as well as do good.

If you were to walk into the boardroom with the aim of influencing your boss on the matter of the plant closure using this strategic story, your focus shouldn't be just on what happened to the four workers. You will also need to share what could potentially happen to the reputation and profitability of the organization if nothing was done to resolve the anticipated safety issues.

Your success will lie in getting your boss to imagine the front page of a newspaper with headlines showing her resignation because of the negligence and losses which have occurred.

Some of you may say, "Of course the bosses will allow the shutting down of the plant to make it safe again with just the story of the four workers. The boss is human, after all, and there's absolutely no need to position the story in a way that shows the negative consequences on organizational reputation and profitability."

But we don't have to search for too long to find examples from other industries that prove that disasters of such nature take place despite warnings. Where the management knew that, if they didn't do something, people's lives could be at risk. The reason the people in power do nothing is because the story in their head is "We can't risk profitability or desired outcomes because a safety issue **may** occur."

Janet Oshiro, Environment, Health and Safety Program Manager at Google, asserts that safety initiatives often interfere with the larger goals of an organization. Safety is a long-term investment that demands time, effort, and monetary investment for the necessary controls to be implemented. The story that people tell themselves is, "Nothing bad will happen to us. So why make these investments?"

That is where storytelling can help, influence, and inspire better decisions. But not just any storytelling, because that would lead to you becoming a storytelling victim.

Storytelling Victims

I come across many corporate professionals who have become victims of storytelling, for all that's been written on the subject. They know stories have the power to engage, influence, and inspire, yet this is only half the lesson of storytelling.

For close to two decades, we have made the case for storytelling in business. The existing literature of business storytelling has done a great job of explaining *why* stories should be told and *how* they should be told. Yet there's a huge gap when it comes to discussing *who* the storytelling is for in the corporate world.

It's this gap that has created storytelling victims. Corporate professionals who tell stories find themselves saying the following after their attempt at storytelling:

- "I told a story and my boss said, 'Get to the point!'"
- "I told a story, and my colleague said, 'What exactly do you want me to do?'"
- "I built a robust narrative but couldn't get employees to embrace the change. As a result, I didn't get the new role I was hoping to get."

However, there's a solution …

Strategic Storytelling

The solution goes beyond just storytelling. It is called *strategic storytelling*. A strategic story, built with immense focus on whom the story is for, has the power to change storytelling outcomes for both individuals and organizations.

This type of storytelling ensures you understand the worldviews of your audience better than they do themselves. The word *strategic* is often perceived as doing something clever and smart but when I decided to call this book *Strategic Storytelling* my intention was simply to make this crucial point: **Only when you have a deep understanding of your audience(s) can you develop the right story.**

In this book, being strategic has less to do with being clever and more to do with understanding the worldviews of your audiences.

The world of consumer marketing has done a great job of deepening our understanding of the worldviews of audiences and shaping stories to make a connection. Think of that shampoo commercial which shows a young woman radiating confidence because her hair is so shiny, silky, and smooth. The marketing storyteller understands that the product isn't just meant to improve someone's hair, but to give them confidence. But somehow the corporate world has not yet embraced the lessons at scale, available to them when it comes to internal communication purposes:

- We keep telling stories which don't resonate with our audience and therefore we don't get an action.

- The current style of storytelling practiced in the corporate world is heavily influenced by social media, and this doesn't work.

- Many of us are made to believe that it's only when we have a leadership role that we can tell stories, but that's far from truth.

The current mess in corporate storytelling is a result of the fact that we don't start with the right question: *Who is storytelling for?* This is the point I want to make, and this is the story I want to tell. However, If you diligently ask, "Who is storytelling for?" you will prioritize a story that resonates over a story that is remarkable.

Who Is This Book For?

It's only fair, in the light of the question above, that I make it clear who this book is for, too.

In essence, it's for corporate professionals. I want every story I share in this book to make you say, "*Now* I understand my problem." I want your heart to beat a little faster. I want your eyes to light up and for you to act in a different way—by telling stories that can drive your success. Not just any old stories but *strategic* stories that have the power to give you the next promotion, role, or responsibility you have always wanted. There's only one thing I am interested in achieving through this book—*your success.*

And your success is just a strategic story away.

My hope is that when you are successful with storytelling, you will be in a position to do things to make the planet and society better, too. Only then can we make the real change happen.

Con un abrazo muy fuerte
Anjali

Why Is Strategic Storytelling Unique?

● ● ●

There is much published on storytelling, but little of it helps corporate professionals avoid becoming storytelling victims. There are many kinds of storytelling, but one for corporate professionals where the focus is tightly on *who the story is for* is missing. In other words, advice on storytelling abounds, but strategic storytelling for corporate professionals is missing. In its absence, corporate professionals naively draw lessons from what is easily accessible to tell a story and thereby become storytelling victims.

Let's explore how many of us have become storytelling victims by exploring the various kinds of storytelling, including the one that's missing. As you read through these, you will start to make connections with your own experiences and understand why the story you've been telling hasn't worked.

1. The Social Media Story

I share my weekly vlog *Thank God It's Story Saturday* on my social media platforms. In 2021, I told the story of Kathrine Switzer (born 1947), the first woman to run a marathon. I've taken her story from her memoir *Marathon Woman: Running the Race to Revolutionize Women's Sports*.

> *It all started in mid-December 1966. It was cold, it was snowing, and Kathrine had just finished running with her coach, Arnie Briggs. Briggs was usually a nice guy, but that day they'd got into a heated argument.*

The backstory to the argument is this: 19-year-old Kathrine was a journalism student in New York. Where she lived, or anywhere she was aware of, there were no running groups for women. So, she joined the cross-country team for men, and Arnie was the coach for this team.

Arnie had run 15 Boston marathons (if you are a runner or have any interest in running, you'd know what a big deal that is!). Every time Arnie would cajole Kathrine into doing especially hard training sessions, he would tell her stories about the Boston Marathon.

One day she said to him, "I'm so sick of listening to these stories! Can't I just run the Boston Marathon?" Arnie looked back at her and said, "No woman ever ran a marathon! They just aren't strong enough." He rejected her request but also said, "If there's a woman who can run a marathon, Kathrine, it's going to be you, but you're going to have to prove it to me during the training that you can do it."

The training continued, and Kathrine proved to Arnie she could run the marathon. They decided to register for the race. They checked the rules and made sure there was nothing mentioned about gender. They found nothing. Kathrine registered using just her initials: K. V. Switzer.

On April 19, 1967, they were there ready for the race. There was a huge buzz about there being a woman at the race. But the fun and excitement lasted only for the first four miles, after which a bus drew up alongside the runner with reporters, journalists, and photographers inside. Among them was this guy wearing an overcoat and a felt hat. He said something to Kathrine which she couldn't quite hear, though it was clearly something not very pleasant.

Then, a few minutes later, she heard the noise of leather shoes on the pavement. It was a very different sound from rubber running shoes. It was the same guy who had been in the bus except this time he was right behind her, grabbing for her running bib—number 261— which she was proud of, in an attempt to remove her from the race. Kathrine managed to escape. Kathrine's boyfriend and fellow runner, Thomas Miller, a 236-pound ex-American footballer, pushed the guy to the ground, and she continued to run.

Kathrine was really stressed after this, and she told Arnie something like: "I don't know where you stand on this, and I've clearly got you into a lot of trouble today, but I will finish this race even if I have do it on my hands and knees. If I stop today, then the thinking that women can't run marathons will be proved right, and I want to prove this thinking wrong."

Arnie suggested to Kathrine they should reduce the pace, continue running and not worry about the distance. As they were running, the same bus went ahead of them and on the bus was Jock Semple, the race manager, the same guy who had conducted the initial assault on Katherine. From the bus Jock said, "You cannot run this marathon. Women don't run marathons and you are in big trouble."

Kathrine worried throughout the race. Later, on top of the worry came the pain, the bruises, the blisters, and the blood. But she was determined to get to the finish line. And she did: Kathrine had changed the history for women in sports.

This story got a great response on social media platforms, with plenty of likes and comments. It's a very human story about overcoming adversity. We love this kind of storytelling because it leverages character and human emotion, and it's in line with every Hollywood and Bollywood movie. However, the probability of this story being useful for driving results in a corporate setting are close to zero, unless, of course, you are giving a speech about equity for women in the workforce. It works well on social media, but it's not one for your boardroom.

Stories that work on social media almost always fail in corporate boardrooms. And there's a further problem: We tend to believe that what we see on social media is what storytelling is. And in a way it is, only not for most corporate boardrooms, which have a very different audience than social media.

Let's not forget that the success metrics for social media storytelling are reach, likes, shares, and comments. Success metrics for corporate storytelling, by contrast, are revenue and profit or, put simply, making the desired change happen in a corporate setting. Mostly the proposition of a social media story is entertainment built for mass, but the proposition of a corporate story is to get people to act. It is worth remembering that entertainment may lead to laughter, joy, or some other emotion but it doesn't guarantee action. A story on social media thrives on reach; a corporate story thrives when it resonates and moves people to action. This is an important distinction.

2. The All-Important External Audience

Many books have been written filled with advice about using story-telling for sales and marketing, exploring stories to draw in customers, investors, and website visitors. These stories can be very important, but there are three unique things about this kind of storytelling that we need to be aware of.

FIRST, MASTERY OF THIS KIND OF STORYTELLING ONLY GETS YOU TO A CERTAIN LEVEL OF SUCCESS IN A CORPORATE SETTING
Let me explain this using a personal experience.

In 2006, I was working in Australia as an associate director of sales with a hospitality brand. I was good at my job because I was a good storyteller, getting clients to buy. Around this time, the director of sales position came up for grabs, and I thought I had it in the bag. To my shock, when the promotion was announced, it was given to someone who didn't contribute even 1 percent toward overall sales. I was aghast at the time, but in retrospect this missed opportunity became a great lesson in my life.

The leadership's justification for not giving me a promotion was that they needed more strategic clout in the leadership and more sales on the ground, and as my boss pointed out, "You're an excellent salesperson. We want you to keep selling and not get bogged down with leading the team." What he was pretty much saying here was: "If I make you the chief, I will lose my best Indian." Exactly the same happened the following year.

What I have learned about being a master storyteller for external audiences—such as the potential customers I converted into sales—is that it doesn't guarantee you will climb the corporate ladder. It can be a catalyst for getting you noticed but it won't necessarily drive your success as a leader. The bitter truth is that, even if you are excellent at telling stories to the external audience and driving results, there comes a point in your career where you should be able to gain a position of higher authority in the organization. We all know someone in the corporate world who's successful with customers but not really considered leadership material. I know this too well, I was one of them for a long time.

SECOND, THE CHOICE THAT THE EXTERNAL AUDIENCE HAVE

Most of the time, telling a story to customers, website visitors, and investors is nonconfrontational in nature because the audience has a choice. If the audience isn't inspired, they won't buy, won't invest, or will leave your website. But the chances of someone questioning the story you're telling is rare because the audience has a choice to accept it or not.

THIRD, BETWEEN THE BOSS AND CUSTOMER, THE BOSS ALWAYS TAKES MORE MINDSHARE

External audiences are important, but a corporate professional rarely wakes up stressing and sweating about a customer. On the other hand, it is not uncommon for us to come across corporate professionals who stress about the fact that their bosses will get upset with them if they lose a customer. It may cost them their promotion. Even when a corporate professional loses a customer, the first thought that runs in her head is:

"What will my boss say?"

This question hounds a corporate professional all the time.

In essence, success with the external audience is important but not enough to drive your success in an organization. Even if you came up with a world-class innovation that can drive success with customers, your boss will need to approve that innovation. Therefore, storytelling to the boss is an important step toward success.

3. The Inspirational Leader

A lot of storytelling advice is aimed at corporate leaders as a way of inspiring team members regarding values and purpose. Mostly, this kind of storytelling mimics theatrical storytelling. It's a little bit like the story about the liquefied natural gas plant I shared in the Preface.

This style tends to leverage the power of personal experiences and lubricates the relationship between the teller and the audience. This style of storytelling is a great tool for building up a leadership brand but isn't necessarily handy when the boss walks into the boardroom and says, "You have five minutes to tell me what you want."

It works well for Leadership Series that are commonly run in corporate organizations where the leaders share stories from personal experiences and share their wisdom or for reinforcing behaviors that are right to begin with—like safety comes first! However, this kind of storytelling does not work quite as well when we ask people to stop doing what they are doing and start doing things they don't even think they need. This might be starting to use AI to develop new models or stop using that old CRM system they are very comfortable with and use a new one instead.

Heavy reliance on this kind of storytelling assumes all is well internally:

- That our employees are motivated and ready to work toward making an organization successful.
- That the employees will embrace every organizational change that promises organizational growth and productivity.
- That the only thing we need is inspiration and there is no skepticism among the employees.

This, however, is far from the truth. We know that the inspirational style of storytelling can work well, but the key is finding the right time and place to use it.

4. Influencing Corporate Decision Makers or People We Work with Internally: The One That's Missing!

The audiences and outcomes for the three kinds of stories outlined above are all clear and well understood, but there's a fourth, more astute type of storytelling in business, and it's for a much tougher audience. How you tell a story to your bosses, employees, peers or cross-functional teams to influence decisions and actions or to bring about change is little understood.

One of the reasons for this is because of the confidential nature of this type of storytelling: No one is going to publish their board presentation on You Tube or share it on social media. Even though there's a lot of information on storytelling, I can confidently say that it's not about this kind!

In *Strategic Storytelling*, we're going to take you to the corporate boardroom where:

- the boss is looking at you and his watch simultaneously, asking you to get to the point
- the team agrees with you on the next change initiative but doesn't align with you
- despite your best efforts, you are failing to achieve healthy levels of diversity, equity, and inclusion in the organization
- despite saying all the right things for an upcoming digital transformation project, your audience has ignored you.

These are stories for places where corporate politics, disbelief, fatigue, and lack of trust exist. The listener is most often someone you see every day, work with every day, and need to align with every day—people, unlike customers, investors, website visitors, or external speech attendees, you can't just leave.

Strategic Storytelling wants to set you up for success in front of your toughest audiences:

- those who can negatively influence your chances of a promotion despite your good work
- those who see you as a good worker but not as a good leader
- those who stop you from being a part of an amazing project that will make the leadership team take notice of you.

Through each of its three parts, *Strategic Storytelling* will help you to drive your success. In each part, I will suggest storytelling identities that corporate professionals like you can adopt.

Eventually, the desired identity of a corporate professional is that of a changemaker, but in the process of becoming a changemaker you need to adopt various other storyteller identities.

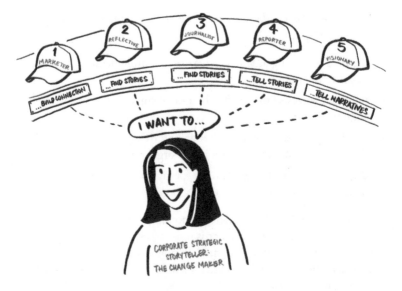

Figure 0.1 Identities of the corporate strategic storyteller:
the changemaker

Figure 0.1 is a visual representation of the key message of this book. Imagine yourself as the person in this figure whose ultimate identity as a corporate strategic storyteller is to be the changemaker, someone who uses stories to make change happen. Your ultimate identity is the one you will wear like a uniform each day with pride. In a corporate setting, the change could be:

- making an organization more data-driven
- making an organization embrace diversity, equity, and inclusion
- making an organization adopt digital transformation by use of exponential technologies
- making an organization build sustainable working models to help planet and society
- making the organization implement mental health and wellbeing initiatives.

However, in the process of becoming a changemaker you will adopt various other storyteller identities. Think of these identities as different caps you can wear to fulfill different purposes in the process of making change happen. Which cap you wear when is determined by the purpose at hand:

To build connections you can adopt the identity of a *marketer storyteller*, who makes the change happen by having a deep understanding of who the story is for.

To find stories, you can adopt the identity of a *reflective and journalist storyteller*.

To tell stories, you can adopt the identity of a *reporter storyteller* who can tell the stories well. This is about *delivery* of the story versus *finding* the story.

To create narratives, to move people in the desired direction, you will wear the visionary cap.

I will cover all these identities in detail in this book.

In *Strategic Storytelling* your journey to success as a strategic storyteller is set out in three parts, showing you how you can adopt key identities along the way.

Part I: Who Is The Story For?
Become a Marketer Storyteller

This part will dive deep into the kinds of audience you come across in the corporate world and why truly understanding them is what creates the difference between whether your story is strategic or not.

We will decode words like *emotion, empathy, resonance,* and *connection,* each of which is important, packed with meaning, but often used loosely and rarely understood.

You will learn to master the art of changing the story to suit various kinds of audience in the corporate ecosystem: bosses, peers, and employees.

Consciously tailoring a story to suit our audience seems logical, but an unconsciously blurred understanding of our audience is common. For example, you are an employee working for a multinational headquartered in Europe. You are telling the story of an amazing project you successfully implemented in Europe to a government (in this case your audience) in Asia. You are proud of the work you have done. The story is sticky for you, but the government official listens to you and says, "It's a great story but it doesn't help our agenda in any way." In that moment you realize that the story is only sticky for you. This happens because stories are often sticky but not necessarily sticky for everyone. The stickiness of the story is subjective. Sticky in this context refers to the potency of the story.

The two things that potentially went wrong here are:

- We got so caught in sharing the story of our project's success that we forgot to tie that back into how that helped the government.
- The desires and the aspirations of government in Europe are different from those in the government in Asia. And we failed to dig deep and understand our audience. We just assumed every government wants similar outcomes.

You feel like you have a good story, and you could tell it to anyone, anywhere, and it would work well. This is true for stories built for a mass audience, but corporate audiences are specific and here you must prioritize connection over attention when storytelling. The difference is that, while you may get someone's attention, attention doesn't necessary lead to an action. An action is the result of connection, and that goes much deeper.

In this part of the book, I suggest you adopt the identity of a **marketer storyteller**. By marketing here, I don't mean the term as it is generally defined—the action or business of promoting and selling products or services. We are looking at the identity of the marketer storyteller as defined by Seth Godin in his book *This is Marketing: You Can't be Seen until You Learn to See*, where marketing is the generous act of helping someone solve a problem. Marketing helps others become who they seek to become.

Don't skip this part thinking it's going to be the same old advice about understanding your audience. I have made that mistake not once but twice, as I'll relate later in the book

Part II: How to Tell a Strategic Corporate Story: *Become a Reflective, Journalist, and Reporter Storyteller*

Having gained a thorough understanding of your audiences, you will now be able to learn how to tell a strategic corporate story. This part debunks a common myth that storytelling is a language of leadership only. The truth is you can be a storyteller from your orientation day. Based on the purpose at hand, you adopt an identity that is most suited to your needs. To find stories you will become either a reflective storyteller who reflects on their own experiences and tell stories based on them, or you become a journalist and find stories to tell that way. *Having* a story is one thing but *telling* it well is another, and as a reporter storyteller you will learn to do just that.

You will learn:

- how to find stories to tell
- what kind of stories work in a corporate setting
- how to structure a story to tell
- the two types of a story structure—maximal and minimal
- how to make a point with a story
- who should tell the story
- how to build a proposition around your story
- the difference between a narrative and a story, as well as when to build which one.

You'll learn how to use these strategies to make your messages stick in conversations, discussions, or presentations.

Part III: How to Tell a Strategic Corporate Narrative: *Become a Visionary Storyteller*

In this part, we will advance our storytelling skills and learn ways to build change narratives—narratives for dynamic changes like digital transformation, diversity, equity, and inclusion. Here you will learn how to adopt and identity of a visionary who can get the audience to stop doing what they are doing because it is not effective anymore, learn new ways of doing things, and imagine a future where they will be successful. The challenge here is to make your audiences believe that they need to change their ways of working.

You will learn:

- why narratives now matter more than ever
- how we miss opportunities to create narratives
- a step-by-step approach to build two types of change narrative:

1. The *maximal change narrative* focuses on explaining why we need funding, resources, and so on for a desired outcome to drive the organization's success. These narratives are rich in nature. They show you where we have come from, what is causing the pressure to change, where are we headed, and, most importantly, how individuals become successful along with their organizations.
2. The *minimal change narrative* focuses on making the audience embrace change wholeheartedly so they and their organization can achieve success. It is not as detailed as the maximal narrative as it doesn't focus on where we have come from and what the pressures to change for a business are. It simply shares where we are now and where we can be.

HOW TO MAKE A SOUND JUDGMENT ON WHICH METHOD TO USE WHEN

The examples in this part are drawn from projects I have personally worked on as well as those that have helped my corporate clients succeed. Through these examples I will show you the nuances of shifting from the theory to the practical. You will learn about the pitfalls that can accompany putting learned methods into practice. In this part, you'll *experience* change happening versus just *learning* how to make change happen.

Corporate professionals have a high degree of responsibility, both internally and externally. Internally, they care deeply about their jobs and their leadership. Externally, they are aware of how many people are watching them, so it matters to them that they do a good job. They're afraid of being replaced because, now more than ever, everyone in the corporate world is anxious about their jobs, so they strive to make themselves indispensable. Typically, they've been doing this by picking up one technical skill after another, but because of skill inflation, the strategy is no longer effective.

For example, I come across many data scientists who are highly skilled and have pushed themselves outside of the comfort zone to gain relevant skills but are unable to make a change happen because they can't tell the right story in the right way to move people in the right direction. Another example related to the recent introduction of corporate professionals with green skills. They are hired because organizations are under a pressure to have green talent, but these corporate professionals are struggling with making a change happen because no one is listening to their suggestions. The crux is, unless you fortify your existing or newly acquired skills with storytelling, you will not be able to make a change happen.

What these people really need to learn is how to be the force behind making a dynamic corporate change happen. And the best way to do this is through strategic storytelling. Strategic storytelling is the universal bridge. While some people are naturally talented at this skill, it is in fact a teachable skill everyone can master to make a dynamic corporate change happen, not only for the good of the organizations they work for, of course, but also for themselves.

A little note before we begin…

Now, if you are reading this book, most likely you are a corporate professional who is short on time. I want to make this process easy and enjoyable for you. There are some things I have added to this book that I always wished I had when I found myself torn between wanting to read for personal growth but also had work deadlines looming around me.

- Short chapters with an estimated reading time given at the start of each chapter. The shortest chapter is three minutes' reading time and the longest 17 minutes. I have used http://niram.org/read/ to calculate the estimated reading time of each chapter. To get the best out of the book, I suggest you read one chapter a day and have a set time of the day when you read it. I usually read first thing in the morning. You could finish reading the book in 26 days, with a maximum of 17 minutes a day.
- A pledge at the end of relevant chapters which includes things you should remember and apply.
- A section for reflection at the end.

So, here's a quick review of some important things I have covered so far:

- A strategic story is a story that understands who the story is for.
- In this book the audience for our storytelling is corporate professionals. If you are a filmmaker, social media influencer, or

someone looking for stories to tell on stage alone, don't waste your time reading *Strategic Storytelling*. There are far better books than this for those domains.

- There are three key things you will learn in this book:
  - who strategic storytelling is for
  - how to tell a strategic corporate story
  - how to tell a strategic corporate narrative.

And one more thing, you can't write a book about storytelling without sharing stories. I have shared many stories in the book, but all names and identifying details—other than mine and those in stories that are well-documented and in the public domain—are fictional.

Without further ado, let's begin...

PART I

Who Is the Story For?

Becoming a marketer storyteller

When I think of this part of Strategic Storytelling, *I think of Seth Godin-style storytelling. My learnings in Part I about being a marketer storyteller are the result of my adaption and application of what I have learned from reading many of Seth's books on consumer marketing and attending his Akimbo Workshops, which include the altMBA—a one-month online workshop.*

Figure 1.1 Marketer storyteller who builds a connection to make a change happen with stories

CHAPTER 1

Correct Alone Doesn't Connect

• • •

Estimated reading time: 7 minutes

A lesson in storytelling that is rarely learned the first time around.

While I was in high school, I lost a debating competition. I was devastated, especially because, before the results were announced, so many people had told me I had spoken so well. I was quietly confident the trophy would be mine, but to my shock this didn't happen.

Perplexed, I went to my teacher. I was hoping that she would tell me the results were unfair, that I deserved the trophy. Well, at least, this was the story I wanted to hear. I wanted, so badly, for someone else to tell me what I believed.

As I walked into the staffroom and made eye contact with my teacher. She excused herself to the other teachers, came to the doorway where I was standing looking so sad, and gave me a big hug. Then she looked straight into my eyes and said, "The results were fair. You *spoke* well but the person who won the trophy *communicated* well." I was confused—so confused I didn't say a word. With a long face, I dragged my feet back to the classroom to nurse my wounds, still not understanding what she meant.

But today I understand exactly what she meant, and that my teacher was giving me my first lesson in storytelling. I can look back and clearly see that I should have adopted the identity of a marketer storyteller to understand that my audience was more than just a group of people listening to me rattle out complicated English words and making superficially correct statements. Looking back, I have to confess, I used those complicated English words to make myself sound intelligent. But what a wrong choice that turned out to be! One that revealed how little I understood my audience.

Here is what I eventually learned:

It takes more than being correct to communicate successfully.

Yes, make your messages correct; from our schooldays on, we're taught to do so. But being correct is just a given. Our key differentiating factor is in how we make these correct messages connect with our audiences.

Understand this:

- Telling a child "Don't eat too much sugar" is a correct message.
- Telling an employee "If we don't change our ways of working, we'll lose market share" may be a correct message in your case.
- Telling consumers "Our product uses only the finest ingredients" (when it really does) is a correct message, too.

But all the above statements rarely lead to the desired action:

- Kids don't stop eating sugar.
- Employees don't jump up and instantly change their ways of working.
- Consumers won't instantly be standing in line to buy your product.

Why not?

Because the story we've told ourselves is that being correct when communicating is enough. However, what we've forgotten is that, if something is correct but doesn't connect, it's incapable of making a change happen. In the past when information was not readily available, your experience would lead to you having more information and knowledge. There was a certain level of respect for those with experience, knowledge, and information, but today access to knowledge and information is not experience dependent. Therefore, our ability to make a change happen is dependent more on our ability to make a connection.

The ability to make a connection is a rare skill today.

Connection only happens when you have a deep understanding of who your message is for. If the job of your communication is to make a connection, then storytelling is your best tool to do it.

The word *connection* is understood to be like one of those emotions which you can't be intentional about. It either happens or it doesn't. But connection in communication can be understood and applied. It's a genuine, not a manipulative, skill. A skill that needs to be constantly honed. A skill that makes you think harder about who your message is for.

Let's explore a common mistake made about connecting with your audience.

A Common Mistake Made about Connection

Imagine you want to develop a knowledge bank that stores all the information your director needs to give answers to shareholders in meetings. You know that the shareholders can ask very specific questions like:

- How much fund was allocated for task A?
- What was the time it took to conclude project C?
- When exactly did we get the information on return on investments made for project Y?

It's not feasible for your boss to remember all this, so a knowledge bank in the form of a framework on a device would be the perfect solution: All your boss would have to do is type in what they are looking for in the search function and they will get a response.

To build the knowledge bank you need funding. To get the funding, you prepare a presentation for your boss. The presentation slides highlight the following content:

- **The problem:** Inability to answer questions during shareholder meetings because there's no immediate access to all the information required.
- **The solution:** The knowledge bank.

This approach is logical, and it's the one commonly practiced by corporate professionals. However, if we were to doff a marketer storyteller's cap here, we would have a different way of communicating the need for the knowledge bank: Rather than solving a problem, we would aim to solve the emotion associated with the problem—your boss's embarrassment at not knowing the answers to shareholders' questions off the cuff.

We have an opportunity here to take our boss back to the last shareholder presentation where they felt embarrassed because they were not able to answer the questions asked, and we can best do this by storytelling. (By the way, don't hesitate to bring up that last stakeholder meeting just because you don't want to embarrass the boss by reminding them of the situation they faced! Make the embarrassment shared, too, by using inclusive phrases like "We were embarrassed that we couldn't answer the questions but also baffled as to how we can be expected to remember specific information of that nature.") Even if such an incident has not taken place, we can still take our boss to an *imaginary* scenario where they were asked a question and were not able to answer.

The *simulation* of the experience via storytelling is the key to making your boss feel the embarrassment. On your part, it demonstrates how deeply you understand the situation and the need to make a change happen. When the knowledge bank takes the embarrassment away, the story resonates, the connection is built, and the action is taken. And you have essayed your role as a marketer storyteller well.

After a decade of working with corporate professionals on storytelling, my biggest lesson has been that our time-poor corporate world doesn't give us the time and mental capacity to dig deep enough to explore the complexities of the worldviews of our audience. We settle with what is obvious to us about our audience, and this often leads to undesired outcomes. We have to build our muscle to become a better marketer storyteller to drive our success. As a marketer storyteller, you need to dig deep to understand your audience's worldviews and psychographics.

It's a lesson that can be learned only by trial and error. Despite being taught the importance of making a connection in school, very early in my life, I didn't really see the wisdom in the lesson until 2014 when I became a "storytelling victim" due to the connection conundrum.

So what is the connection conundrum? We'll find out in Chapter 2 after taking our pledge to remember and apply what we've learned in Chapter 1.

I pledge to remember and apply the following lessons:

- If the goal of my communication is to make a connection, then storytelling is my best tool to do it.
- My communication cannot just be *correct*; it also has to *connect*.
- I must never assume I know my audiences well. I must try to understand their emotions, create resonance, build connection, and then drive the desired action. That's what a true marketer storyteller does.
- Storytelling is not about solving the problem per se but solving the negative emotion associated with the problem.

Now let's move on to the connection conundrum.

CHAPTER 2

The Connection Conundrum

• • •

Estimated reading time: 15 minutes

A hard lesson in storytelling

It's September 2014. I've had one of those nights where I went to bed early thinking I would wake up refreshed, but my underlying anxiety wouldn't let me rest. I've tossed and turned endlessly. I was thinking about my early flight to Kuala Lumpur. I was to give a keynote on corporate storytelling to a large audience.

I check the alarm clock every ten to fifteen minutes for hours. I'm worried I'll sleep through the alarm. I stare at the clock as it ticks over from 3:59 to 4:00 a.m. The alarm starts ringing.

With my daughter in mind, I've chosen an early flight so I will have more time with her in the evening. Getting home early will allow me to tell her a bedtime story—otherwise, all I get to do is to tell corporate ones! (Though let me set the record straight—bedtime stories and corporate stories are very different.)

I go about my morning routine. As I'm getting ready, I am still feeling unsettled. I go to the kitchen table to check the schedule I've arranged for my daughter's day: school drop-off, pickup, playdate, and meals. All covered!

My thoughts turn to my keynote speech: Am I prepared? Am I organized?

I reach the airport on time and get through security in less than 20 minutes (yes, in Singapore you can do that). I arrive in Kuala Lumpur in just 45! But after that, things take a nosedive.

I am met with long immigration lines. Then the horrendous traffic makes me wonder if I will make it to the venue on time. All the subtleties of my talk are banished from my mind.

My palms are sweaty as if I've just finished a long run. I fumble with my phone trying to find the organizer's number. The phone's touchscreen won't work because of my sweaty hands. I wipe my hands on my black dress. Oops, now I have a makeup smear on the dress.

When I reach the organizer I tell them, "I'm here in Kuala Lumpur and will get to the venue as soon as I can." My heart is racing, and I'm already thinking about how I could make it up to the organizers if I don't get there punctually.

Somehow, I reach the venue just in time. I run up to the sound engineer so he could ready me for the stage. The stage manager is frustrated because the dress I'm wearing makes it hard to hook the mic up. One more thing to ratchet up my anxiety!

I try to shake it off and try to compose myself. But then the stage manager snaps at me to take off my earrings because they're interfering with the mic sound. I'm getting frustrated.

I am running a constant mantra over and over in my mind, "You've got this. Stay calm. You've got this. Stay calm." The mantra is still running when, five minutes into my talk, one of the heels on my shoes breaks. I almost fall over but, having steadied myself, take off both my shoes.

Then the mantra stops, and a new louder voice is in my head. It's so loud it could be a megaphone. This voice says, "I'll never get through it all. This is so unfair!"

I give the rest of my talk without my shoes on. Of course, I give a fake laugh to signal to the audience that this experience is as much a funny moment for me as it is for them. But, in my heart, I'm telling myself I want to be a stay-at-home mom forever after this experience.

After my keynote in the morning, in the break every conversation I have is about my broken heel. I laugh along, but internally I'm deeply affected by the mishap: The broken heel has broken my confidence, too. But, of course, it's not just about the heel. It's about feeling like a failure despite my best attempts.

On the short flight back home, I sit on my airplane seat with earplugs, eye shades, and a perfect plan in place. I will sleep for 45 minutes, which is the flight time, and then spend a wonderful evening with my daughter because I am now feeling guilty about having left her in the first place.

However, I can't sleep, and a question keeps nagging at me: Why, during the morning break, hadn't people talked about the content of my talk or the experiences I'd shared with them in my keynote? I'd worked hard on the talk and gathered a lot of data to make the point I wanted to make. But where was the conversation I was there for and why had my broken heel become so important?

I'm still thinking hard, with my eyes closed under the eye shades, when I hear the flight attendant make the announcement, "Welcome to Singapore, ladies and gentlemen. And to all residents a warm welcome home." I leave the question about the keynote hanging in my head and soon it's replaced with a different kind of question: How can I compensate for the guilt of having left my daughter? A movie, ice cream, a board game ... what shall we do?

This day in my life is a day in many working women's lives. As a story practitioner, telling the story of this day comes naturally to me. The first time I told it was while having a coffee with a client soon after the event. I told the story and said that the point of it was that it showed how I'd been so wracked with guilt about being a working mother that I'd managed to make a fool of myself on stage.

My client corrected me: "You're making the wrong point. The point of this story is that being a working mother can be a deeply personal and testing choice." I nodded in agreement. My client was right. I had to rise above the heels and think of this event's capacity to connect with others.

Soon, this experience became one of staple stories. I've told it often in many engagements, and years later people still ask me about it. People absolutely love this story, but why?

Why Some Stories Stick

Some stories stick because they check the following boxes:

1. The story shows vulnerability, which creates connection—a well-established point in storytelling

This story works because it removes the pretense of perfection and shows me as vulnerable, trying to do it all and yet failing. My story gives people the permission to fail, despite trying hard. The thing about any story really is that, even when it is a personal story, people are looking for themselves in it. It's a bit like a group photograph, where, the moment you set eyes on it, you seek out your own image first.

2. Vulnerability is a strong bridge of connection between people—it gives us permission to be imperfect.

Please also take note that, even though vulnerability is a strong bridge of connection between people, the power of vulnerability starts to fade when a junior employee shows vulnerability. This is well-documented by psychologist Elliot Aronson who tracked the audience's reactions to participants in a game show. When the high-performing contestants spilled coffee on themselves, the audience liked them more. They were competent and relatable. They were human and imperfect. However, when the mediocre performers did the same thing, people liked them less.

This is called the Pratfall Effect. In social psychology, the Pratfall Effect is the tendency for interpersonal appeal to change after an individual makes a mistake, depending on the individual's perceived competence. In particular, highly competent individuals tend to become more likable after committing mistakes, while average-seeming individuals tend to become less likable even if they commit the same mistake.

What this indicates to us is when we reach a certain stage in our careers and are considered high performers, our vulnerability and shortcomings make us more relatable and therefore, more likeable. However, where low to average performers are concerned, the research indicates that there should be a greater focus for them to first gain a certain level of competence before showing vulnerability.

In this story, showing vulnerability works because as the keynote speaker, I am naturally considered credible and highly competent.

3. The story has a specific audience—it is hyper-targeted—which creates resonance.

This story also resonates with a very specific audience—working women. If a story doesn't resonate, it doesn't ring as genuine for the listener, even if it is factual otherwise. When people gasp and say, "Oh, that's so true," it's not because what you are saying is factually correct but because what you are saying resonates with them.

When something resonates with you, it reminds you of an experience you have already had. It aligns with your worldviews.

If a well-told factual story is like glue, a story that resonates is like superglue.

4. It shifts knowledge into understanding for the opposite gender.

This story is interesting to men because it surprises them and makes them ask a question, "How come I've never noticed how our world is designed to suit men?" It would never occur to them to feel parental guilt when giving a keynote speech or worry about their earrings interfering with the mic, let alone having a heel break on them. Of course, men know about the difficulties faced by working women *in theory*, but a story colored by the nitty-gritty of what this means *in practice* can becomes a powerful medium to create real, empathetic understanding.

If the goal is to shift knowledge into understanding for those who can't have the same experiences as you, tell a story. Stories are experience simulators.

5. It's a small-scale story, so it can be an experience many other people can identify with.

Not much happens in this story: I went to a conference, and a few things went wrong. It's not an epic story of climbing Everest or surviving a plane crash. And yet, precisely because of its smallness or everydayness, it's highly resonant.

Something like this could happen to anyone and, sometimes, a few times a day. As a result, a larger group of people can respond: "That's the story of my life." Don't get me wrong: People do give a lot of attention to big stories like surviving a plane crash, but they don't see themselves in those stories. In fact, after listening to a big story, what we really say to ourselves is "This will never happen to me" or "That's got nothing to do with me." We may love Usain Bolt's story and admire him, but few of us dare to be like him.

Big stories are great attention grabbers but weak catalysts for creating a change through the inspiration generated in the story. Small stories have a higher probability of making a change happen.

In a corporate setting we should look for stories with small, unexpected events because our goal is to make a change happen. If we can find a moment with a small unexpected event that resonates with many people, the probability of making a change happen increases. On the other hand, large, unexpected events in a story have high entertainment value and are very suited for making a movie or writing a novel.

In a corporate setting, resonance takes precedence over entertainment.

6. It's a story with multiple unexpected events.

In the story, a few unexpected things happen: I can't get to sleep, there are long immigration lines, my earrings get snagged in the mic, and finally those pesky heels! The story keeps turning up the dial on unexpected occurrences: Just imagine if the story was only about my earrings interfering with the mic; it wouldn't have the same impact.

The impact potential of a small story is often dependent on the number of unexpected events in the story. An event on its own is often not as impactful.

After telling this story repeatedly at different keynote presentations and seeing it perform so well, I *thought* I'd cracked the code of storytelling. Not only did I know how to assemble and develop a story, but I was also able to tell a story well, too. But what was soon to become clear to me was that this was not *strategic* storytelling for all environments.

As someone investing in understanding the practice of storytelling, it's likely that you may be aware of many of these elements in storytelling already. These are some of the early lessons of the story discipline. Yet, the great things I am telling you about this story became the very reasons behind why a client almost came to dislike me and how I came to make one of the biggest faux pas of my career. (This is the moment in this book when you get to understand why *Strategic Storytelling* offers such a unique take on storytelling and how it can drive your success.)

When a Great Story Fails You

I've been invited to work with senior business leaders from a large company.

On the first day, I walk into the room feeling confident, my confidence built on having already run a successful story practice for a few years. There are about 30 people in the room, and the objective is to articulate business messages and build stories around them, just as I've done for many other clients.

To build rapport, I start my presentation with my Kuala Lumpur broken heel story, but I soon notice that there's one gentleman in the audience—let's call him Sam—who seems dissatisfied with my story. Sam is huffing and puffing, he's on his phone a lot, and the look on his face says, "What the hell am I doing here?" He doesn't try to hide what he's feeling at all, and I'm now feeling less confident because Sam is not happy. No matter what I say or do, Sam disagrees with me. Over lunch, I reach out to him and ask how I could make things better for him, but he seems uninterested.

At the end of the event, the organizer tells me that Sam has written an email to all the managers and anyone else who'll be attending my session the next day, stating that mine is the worst session he's attended, and they shouldn't waste their time going to it the next day.

I'm shocked. I don't know what to say. I try to ask Sam what exactly is not worth his time but don't get a clear response. I go to the bathroom, wash my face, and look at myself in the mirror. I don't see a shocked face; I see a face full of doubt and, of course, dribbling eyeliner. I begin to doubt all my past success. I feel like a fake and just hope that what I'm experiencing is just a dream, not a reality. My profession is an integral part of my identity, and I see its value diminishing in front of my eyes.

I feel smaller than small. The session ends, and everyone other than Sam seems happy. I return home but it's a different me: someone who's a lot less confident even if still determined to figure out what happened and why Sam was so unhappy. I am resolved to hunt down the reason but unfortunately no answer surfaces. I keep looking.

Why a Great Story Can Fail You

A couple of months later, I was working on my first large change storytelling consulting project. It was an eight-month-long digital transformation project on which I was working with the CEO of the company directly. The number of people we needed to influence via the story was close to 10,000, including a variety of audiences from employees of different departments, through to partners, customers, and the CEO. I had the core of the story done in a month or so. The leadership team loved it and asked me to get the ball rolling. But when I looked at the core story more closely, I began to wonder why employees of department X or the partners would care about it. In fact, the story worked only for the customers and no one else. I realized that we needed not one core story but many strategic stories tailored for different departments.

I realized, too, it was about the *context* of the connection in storytelling, not just connection per se. I had finally found the answer to the question that had bugged me for the last couple of months. Why had Sam been so unhappy? He was unhappy because the audience he had in mind was not the audience *I* had in mind—customers. The session was designed for the 30 or so people in the room who wanted to tell their story to the customers, but Sam had walked into the session thinking that the story he would build would be for his boss. I wished that, rather than asking him what I could do to make his experience better, I had asked him who exactly he was trying to build his story for? Or even better I wished I had started my work that day with a different statement: Rather than saying we were there to learn storytelling, I should have said we were there to learn storytelling for our customers. That is why when my clients say, "Please work with our teams and teach them storytelling," I respond by saying, "I can teach them storytelling but not strategic storytelling. If you want to learn strategic storytelling we have to hyper-target the story: We need to know who it is for."

When working with Sam, I didn't define who the storytelling was for. *Mea culpa.* I had not worn the hat of a marketer storyteller.

But there's more to this than just being able to define your audience. I call it a *story bias*.

Story Bias

Even when the target audience is well-defined, it's not uncommon for us to default to an entirely different audience. For example, I know from working with C-suite leaders that they are always thinking about the board, investors, and shareholders, and from working with middle management, that they are always thinking about their bosses. Even if they are working on a story for customers, it is common for corporate professionals to say, "Oh, but my boss wouldn't like that story." But we were not building the story for the boss!

You see the pattern here? Everyone wants the best story for the audience who has the power to influence their careers. And so the moment the story fits the default audience they have in mind, they think it's the right story for everyone. It is because in their head they are only seeing the audience they want to see. This is called a *story bias*. We see only the audience we want to serve, even though there's more than one audience in the corporate world. And connection remains a conundrum because we have a story bias that prohibits us from seeing the context of connection.

After taking this chapter's pledge, we'll move on to the next chapter where we will get to understand the subject of context a little more deeply.

I pledge to remember and apply the following lessons:

- Vulnerability is a strong bridge of connection between people. It is permission to be imperfect.
- If a well-told factual story is like glue, a story that resonates is like superglue.
- If your goal is to shift knowledge into understanding for those who can't have the same experiences as you, tell a story. Stories are experience simulators.
- Big stories are great attention grabbers but weak catalysts for creating a change through the inspiration generated in the story. Small stories have a higher probability of making a change happen. A story is big or small depending on the degree of the unexpected events in the story.
- A core story needs to have many strategic stories drawn out of it to make a connection with different kinds of audience.
- We all have a story bias. We only have a certain audience in our mind who we want to tell the story to. If the story works for that audience, we tend to believe it works for everyone. We just don't see the other audiences. They remain invisible to us. Therefore, before you begin building a story, be very clear on who the story is for.

CHAPTER 3

The Context of Connection

• • •

Estimated reading time: 11 minutes

The context of connection is the who, why, and how of connection.

In 2013, soon after I started Narrative: The Business of Stories, my story practice, I was on a flight to London for work when I read in *Daring Greatly* by Dr. Brené Brown that connection, not response, is what makes something better.

This line took me back to a day in 2005 when I was walking up to my boss's office to get his approval on something. Looking at him through the glass window of his office, I could see he was very busy. He had his phone in one hand and was tapping away on his laptop with the other, and there were several papers on his desk. I told myself it was clearly a bad time so I turned on my heels. As I was tiptoeing back to my corner of the office, I heard his voice, "Anjali, come in. I have all the time for you." He closed his laptop flap and started talking to me. In this simple act, he made a clear connection with me and didn't just respond to my needs. It was a connection made through an action: The act of getting up, calling me back, and talking to me. It's not uncommon for us to hear stories about small encounters where a connection was felt: The flight stewardess who brings me a special meal; the waiter who remembers a customer's name on a repeat visit to the restaurant, and so on. The question, though, is how do you make a connection via communication?

The Who, Why, and How of Connection

In communication, it's resonance that creates a connection. The challenging thing, though, is that we can only tell stories that resonate if we understand the who, why, and how of the connection, or in other words understand the context of connection. This may sound like common sense, but if connection were that simple, everyone would communicate and resonate well already.

When you're listening to a speaker tell a story, if the speaker is a good storyteller, it will connect with you, and you will be inspired. The connection happens because of the speaker's story, because of the resonance created, and because you feel seen, heard, and valued. Even if the story isn't about you, you can find yourself in it; it reminds you of a moment you have experienced. It feels like someone has understood your problems and put them into words; that someone is just like you, experiencing similar problems to you.

How you build the connection through creating resonance depends on the context and the outcomes you want. Let's look at a few scenarios to dig deeper into the who, why, and how of the connection.

The Storyteller on Stage

- *Connection—who:* Who is the audience who has come to listen to the talk? Let's assume this is a talk on International Women's Day and women from various organizations have come to listen to the talk.

- *Connection—why:* You want to inspire your audience, to make them feel they *want* to do something and *can* do it. In this case, perhaps you are inspiring them to have a bigger and bolder ambitions despite the challenges they face in the corporate world.

- *Connection—how:* Through a story in which the audience can see themselves. My broken heel story mentioned in the previous chapter will do a good job of building resonance and connection here because a lot of the audiences will connect with it and see themselves in it. This is exactly why Sheryl Sandberg, former chief operating officer at Meta, made a last-minute addition of a story to her TED Talk "Why We Have Too Few Women Leaders." The story was about her daughter clinging to her legs and telling her not to leave home. The story did a brilliant job of connecting with the intended audience. They felt like the speaker was narrating their life.

Stage storytelling generally inspires actions that individuals take that only affects them. For example, a story of fat to fit inspires healthy living which is an individual action; a story of redundancy to reinvention inspires upskilling which is an individual action

However, I don't see myself ever using my broken heel story or Sheryl Sandberg's daughter's story in a boardroom. It doesn't make a connection in the boardroom. In a boardroom the context of the connection is very different.

The Storyteller in the Boardroom

- *Connection—who:* Managers, peers, customers, investors, clients, etc.
- *Connection—why:* You want to influence your audience, to affect or change how they develop, behave, or think.
- *Connection—how:* Through a story which helps your audience achieve their desired outcomes.

If you are my manager listening to me in the boardroom presenting a strategy, you are most likely not listening to me to be inspired. The key to connection in the boardroom is influence—influence that can eventually lead to a desired action.

The way I will make my manager listen to me is by understanding what change she is trying to drive and tell the story in line with that. This is how my manager will feel seen, heard, and valued. For example, senior stakeholders may be pressuring my manager to bring in a certain amount of revenue in the following quarter and ensure we are in line with environment, social, and governance (ESG) requirements at the same time, so it's important I tell a story to help my manager achieve her goal.

In an influencing environment, the decisions that are made affect many people. Therefore, it takes longer to get influence-based outcomes than it takes to get inspiration-based outcomes.

Inspirational storytelling leverages characters and emotions while influential storytelling often leverages analysis and thinking.

If connection is what we seek, then storytelling is the best way to create the connection. However, understanding the who, why, and how of the connection determines whether the storytelling will work or not.

Storytelling connects only if you are laser-focused on the who, why and how. Remember:

A story that works on the stage doesn't work in the boardroom.

A story that works in the boardroom doesn't work in a team meeting.

A story that works in a team meeting doesn't work in a one-to-one team conversation.

A story that works in a one-to-one team conversation doesn't work in a sales one-to-one conversation.

While all stories have the power to move people to act, whether that power comes in to play depends on the context of connection.

Next time you are ready to tell a story, use the table below and dig deep to uncover the context of connection:

Connection—Who	
Connection—Why	
Connection—How (with a story)	*(Here it is important to ask why the story you have selected would resonate?)*

One of the most common mistakes I have seen being made by corporate professionals in terms of storytelling is to use stage-style storytelling or stories they have heard in workshops in the boardroom. It's worth digging into why we like the kind of storytelling that happens in workshops and on stage but fail to effectively use those same stories to drive outcomes in boardrooms—why these stories *sound* so amazing but ultimately are ineffectual.

The Problem Stage and Workshop-Style Storytelling Creates in Boardrooms

You've read several books on storytelling. You've watched YouTube videos, or may even have attended a course on storytelling or heard someone give a fantastic talk filled with stories. You love the stories you've heard and you are yearning to retell those stories. Filled with enthusiasm you walk into a boardroom, tell that story and your boss says, "Get to the point." Ouch, that hurt, but before you decide "No more storytelling for me," let's uncover what happened here. Why didn't your story work?

Most of these platforms, talks, YouTube videos, workshops, books (mostly, not all) advocate using *rich stories*, which can be very engaging. But, ultimately, rich stories are doomed to fail in the boardroom. While they can be very enjoyable, you can't apply them to the real world of work because most of us don't spend our corporate lives on stage. We spend them in boardrooms trying to persuade, convince, and influence other people.

Before the incident with Sam I related in Chapter 2, my technique had always worked because the focus was on *inspiration*—which is the norm for keynotes, workshops, or helping leaders craft change stories. As I have mentioned before, this tends to mimic stage-style storytelling. But Sam that day was looking for a boardroom story that he could tell his boss.

So, if you have gone to a workshop on storytelling or read a book on storytelling, both of which you loved but don't seem able to apply in the boardroom, I am with you. You're not alone. The truth is simple: Inspiration-geared storytelling doesn't work in the boardroom if you are presenting to the boss.

You may well wonder why environments like the workshop and the stage use inspirational-style storytelling at all. It is because we put a premium on being entertained, engaged, and having fun in these environments. No one wants to be a boring speaker or a boring workshop facilitator. The expectation from these environments is: "Engage me, entertain me, and then educate me" (in that order).

Things get even more muddled because we tend to use the words *inspiration* and *influence* interchangeably:

To inspire means to fill (someone) with the urge or ability to do or feel something, especially to do something creative.

To influence means the capacity to have an effect on the character or behavior of someone or something.

Inspiration is more emotion based, while influence is more thinking based.

Why Influencing Is the Better Fit for Corporate Boardrooms

You *influence thinking* but *inspire action*. Making your boss change strategy will require influencing them over a few occasions before they decide to change the strategy, but making your team member use a new digital tool to submit a training request will require inspiring them.

Influence is a lot subtler and a better fit for a corporate boardroom because in corporate boardrooms we often make decisions that can potentially lead to embarrassment, failure, and discomfort. The consequences of the decisions you make impact on a lot more people. Inspiration works well on stage because individuals take action that has consequences only for themselves, as mentioned earlier.

Stage-type, inspiration-geared storytelling is all around us because we see it being practiced at events or when watching speeches online. On the other hand, the presentations and stories that are meant to influence in corporate boardrooms aren't readily available for outsiders to see. What are the chances you will see a boardroom presentation on YouTube? And this lack of access to corporate storytelling also becomes the reason behind the lack of adoption of strategic storytelling. While we have plenty of examples of storytelling in action at our disposal, we do not, as yet, have many examples of strategic storytelling in the boardroom.

It's worth keeping in mind that we've become quite good at using storytelling when addressing customers and investors because we value sales or investment. The reason we are telling the story is very clear to us. The same level of awareness is missing when we tell a story in a corporate setting to our bosses, peers, and team members. Storytelling to the external audience is well documented, and the context of making a connection with that audience is often clear. Because we are so outward-focused, we forget that outward success is impossible without an inward focus.

I am sure by now you are thinking: "So what does happen in a corporate boardroom? You've told us what *doesn't* work in the boardroom, but what kind of story *does* work there?"

In the next chapter, after taking our pledge in this one, we'll go into the corporate boardroom and find out.

I pledge to remember and apply the following lessons:

- You can only create a connection when you understand the context of the connection.
- The context of connection is about understanding the who, why, and how of the connection.
- There are stories to inspire and stories to influence.
- Influence is the capacity to change thinking; inspiration is the capacity to fire action.
- Because there are a lot more negative emotions associated with the decisions we make in the boardroom, we must use influence to shape decisions in the boardroom. Inspiration is more emotion-based, while influence is more thinking-based.
- Influencing our audience is a better strategy for a boardroom because the decisions we make affect a lot more people. Our responsibility is so much greater.

Now let's get to that corporate boardroom.

CHAPTER 4

Welcome to the Corporate Boardroom

* * *

Estimated reading time: 9 minutes

How to make a choice between maximal and minimal stories.

Corporate settings can demand a maximal (rich) or a minimal (spare) story, depending on the situation. Let me explain what I mean by a maximal and a minimal story using a scenario.

Maximal and Minimal Stories

Let's say an organization that manufactures specialist pet medication is about to launch a training program for its staff to equip them with the skills to educate a key distribution partner or a veterinary practitioner about one of their products. Here are the ways the person who announces the training program can talk about it:

OPTION 1: NO STORY
"We have a pressing agenda item. We must make our distribution channel aware of the correct use of our products. Hence, we will be rolling out a training program for our staff to learn how to run the education program."
The statement made by the project lead, announcing the launch of the training program, is plain and straightforward—all we get is an objective fact. The announcement has stripped away any emotion and, in doing so, any real connection. Communication is about the transfer of emotions and occurs when something I say to you moves you to act. By communicating with such utter objectivity, I am merely passing on

information and there's nothing to move people into acting. Put simply, there's a big gap between receiving information and taking an action.

In option 1, the method of cascading information is this:

Here's the problem or the information: We need to educate veterinary professionals.

Here's the solution or the desired action: Let's run a training program.

Sadly, this stripped-back objectivity is the most common option adopted by corporate professionals. We adopt an objective style because we are focused on efficiency: Let's get this over with in the quickest possible way. It's as if we are still living under the conditions of the Industrial Revolution where productivity and efficiency were prized over everything else, when what we have today is a connection economy where efficiency has become secondary, since people look for meaning in their work.

As we move more and more into situations like remote, hybrid, and online working, in which people can decide on their own about how much effort, attention, and care they put into their work, choosing objectivity for efficiency's sake is a mistake. A project lead can correct course by creating a connection with the staff by using story. They now have two options: the maximal and minimal story.

OPTION 2: A MAXIMAL STORY FOCUSING ON INSPIRING ACTION

"Last week, our call center received a call from a distressed dog owner and father, Marcel. He had administered the medication on his 7 year old beloved family dog. The dog had started convulsions and vomiting. Marcel was panicking and wasn't sure what was going on. Our customer care officer urged Marcel to take the dog to the clinic immediately. Marcel dashed to the emergency vet.

You can just imagine the family's worry and difficulty in being unable to reassure the children about what was happening.

The vet nurse took the dog from Marcel and returned 15 minutes later. The dog was fast asleep and healthy.

The dog was fine, but on later learning Marcel's story, we were not. We were, in fact, alarmed. We needed to figure out what had happened. After an investigation, we realized there are two specific areas where we have to be mindful of when prescribing our product for dogs with existing neurological conditions. One of those things was missed by the veterinary practitioner while prescribing the product.

As we dug deeper into the problem, we realized we have had 32 calls over the last week indicating that the prescription of the product is not taking place accurately in terms of dosage and pets with other existing conditions.

Clearly, we as an organization need to educate our teams and remind veterinary practitioners on ways to do this better.

Here we are, slogging away every day to make our brand a chosen brand in the profession, but lack of education and knowledge about the accurate prescription of the product can undermine our efforts and put animals lives and veterinary businesses at risk. All our hard work can count for nothing if we don't educate the veterinary practitioners."

Now, this is a well-developed "big" story. In telling it, you'll probably get physiological reactions back from your audience such as gasps and sighs. Such responses confirm that a connection has formed between the teller and the listener. A physiological reaction is often a confirmation that connection has taken place.

The listeners will become part of the story by expressing their emotions such as disappointment or frustration. They may even share ways to make the program better. And when they do this, it's a confirmation they are invested in the outcome. They are listening and they care. They are inspired to act. They feel for the people and clients involved and for their efforts being wasted.

Now let's move on to a new audience for your message about the program—the boardroom. You now need to convince the bosses to let you run this training program. The story you told earlier to employees was to inspire them to sign up for the training program, but the outcome you need from your bosses is to approve the training budget. The previous story won't work as effectively in this scenario. Option 3 shows how the story might shift when telling it to the bosses who you want to approve the funds.

OPTION 3: A MINIMAL STORY FOCUSING ON INFLUENCING A DECISION

"Last week a veterinary practice failed their client and almost killed a beloved family pet because our distribution channel was unable to educate our customers on the appropriate use of our products.

Transcriptions of customer-care hotline calls reveal we have received more than 32 calls last week alone, together indicating a lack of knowledge on the use of our products by our distribution channel. This is both shocking and alarming. This incident clearly demonstrates that what is at stake here is our brand reputation—our identity as a company that produces products for health and planet.

As a result, we are going to introduce a training program for our staff on how best to educate our distribution channel on the appropriate use of our products. I request that you consider approving a XX budget for the training rollout."

We typically tell stories to inspire, engage, motivate, and influence. But when it comes to communicating with management, you must drop the first three. They run the company. If you need to inspire, engage, and motivate them, you're in trouble!

The only thing I focus on when telling a story to management is to influence the decision-making.

Now, a question worth asking is…

What Kind of Stories Influence Management?

What kind of a story can I tell to influence a management decision? These are minimal (spare) stories that help with:

- **TIME:** saving time
- **IMAGE:** making an organization you work for look good or in other words enhance its reputation. Environmental, social, and governance (ESG) standards are a big part of this.
- **MONEY:** reducing cost or making profit

I often ask my clients, "Is this a story for TIM?" TIM is just an abbreviation for time, image, and money. When it comes to finding a story that will influence management, I look for one that is filled with insight and has a potential to influence.

Here's a summary of the differences between the three options:

WELCOME TO THE CORPORATE BOARDROOM

	Aims at	Time taken to tell the story (estimated)	Are characters used to communicate?	Series of events	Emotion for connection	Key focus
Option 1 No story	Complete objectivity	30 seconds	No character used	Not applicable	No use of emotion	What needs to be done
Option 2 Maximal story (*inspires*)	Making people *feel* the problem for others and for themselves	2–3 minutes	Character is at the heart of this story and a key way in which feelings are created. (Please take note in the case above that the characters include not only the family but also the employee whose efforts are wasted.)	2–3	Focuses heavily on emotions	Making people take action by deciding for themselves
Option 3 Minimal story (*influences*)	Explaining what is at stake if the desired action is not taken	1 minute	Character is mentioned but in a subtle manner	1–2	Subtle use of emotions	Save the brand's reputation and approve the budget

43

How Stories Can Be Made Minimal

Notice how the stories told to bosses in option 3 have the following characteristics:

They are concise: We can make stories concise by reducing the number of events, just as in the aforementioned case. In option 3, we have mentioned only the call from Marcel and then 32 other calls (so two events). Mentioning the events adds credibility, and the data added further solidifies the case. This gives insight into your narration and helps keep the focus on the point that matters or that will build the desired connection. In option 2, by contrast, we have more events, which invites the audience to become part of the story, build a connection, and become invested in the outcome.

They are task oriented: When the story is task oriented, the focus is more about doing something than about the problem itself. Unlike option 1 where we go straight from problem to solution, in option 2 we get to know a lot about the problem—what happened to Marcel, his family and their pet—before offering the solution. In option 3, there's yet another approach: "This happened, which was a problem, because it puts this at stake (TIM), so now let's do this." There's a clear focus on each cause and effect in the chain.

The focus is on the point and not on the character. In option 3, we focus on the point we are making, and we have a very clear action. In option 2, our role is not to tell people what to do, but to get them to *want* to do what is being proposed in the story. No doubt we are telling Marcel's story, but our focus is on the point and not just making people feel sorry for Marcel, the dog, his children and themselves. A well-developed character in the story might create the risk of removing the focus from the point of the story and leave the audience caught in the emotion of the character.

Management is primarily interested in ways you can assure that performance will be unlocked, because this is how the organization becomes successful. It is management's core responsibility.

Some of you may be raising eyebrows at this point and thinking that management does care about people and that I'm not right in asserting that management cares more about profit. If that is your situation, fantastic! You can still benefit if you continue reading and I promise that you will become even better at telling stories that can unlock performance, unlock people, and unlock ways you can make the planet and society better.

I want to remind everyone reading that when you work with people you have to *unlock people, who* then unlock *performance.* This is how people and organizations become successful. Stories can help you drive corporate success.

When I advocate storytelling as a tool to corporate professionals, I have to demonstrate an understanding of their world: That corporate professionals live in a busy, fast-changing and time-poor world. How, then, can we accelerate the process of gaining storytelling skills for a corporate professional?

A lot of the inefficient practices in corporate storytelling happen because we don't have the appropriate vocabulary for supporting our storytelling. In the next chapter, after this chapter's pledge, we'll turn to the crucial issue of acquiring and using the right storytelling vocabulary.

I pledge to remember and apply the following lessons:

- Depending on who you are telling a story to in a corporate environment, you will need to make your story either maximal or minimal. A maximal story is one that is well developed, while minimal means it is spare (less detailed) in nature.
- Minimal stories are concise and task oriented and focus on the point more than the characters in the story.
- For leaders, the stories that show organizational success are important because that is the role they have in the organization. They are directly responsible for making sure the organization succeeds. Therefore, stories that focus on TIM (time, image, and money) work well for leadership. They succeed when they can show the organization is succeeding.
- For employees, you must show their success. For example, if you tell an employee to do something because it leads to the organization becoming efficient, the employee will not be as enthused; however, if you ask the employee to do something that makes them efficient and as a result gives them the time to be part of a team that is leading innovation in the organization, then their enthusiasm will shine through. Their success leads to organizational success, but you need to find their success in the success of the organization

---

Now let's learn something about the vocabulary of storytelling.

CHAPTER 5

The Vocabulary of Storytelling

• • •

Estimated reading time: 7 minutes

Words matter.

A client might say to me:

Oh, I feel so confused with storytelling. What's the focus? Is it empathy, resonance, worldviews, connection? And what exactly do these words mean anyway? I'm a time-poor corporate professional who is under immense pressure to drive results. I was told storytelling can help me achieve results, but I feel lost in the sea of words.

They are right, of course: There are so many words associated with storytelling, but often they only sow confusion. To ensure this confusion was experienced widely and not just felt by a few people (including me), I started asking my clients random questions about the vocabulary of storytelling, including:

- What is a connection?
- What are worldviews?
- What is empathy?
- What is resonance?

All too often, words like these were used interchangeably and so caused confusion, hampering our efforts to make a meaningful connection via our storytelling efforts. Let me ask you a few questions around storytelling and thus demonstrate how we can easily get lost in the words we use.

"What does storytelling achieve?"

You might respond to this question in a variety of ways:

Storytelling builds connection.

Storytelling creates resonance.

Both answers are correct but are not interchangeable.

"How can we tell the best stories?"

By making sure we understand our audience's worldviews.

By making sure we demonstrate empathy.

Once again both are correct but not interchangeable.

A meaningful connection with storytelling is almost impossible without a clear vocabulary. Vocabulary helps you establish a process for building a strategic story. I will use all four words (or related ones)—connection, resonance, worldviews, and empathy—in one short paragraph and then deep-dive into each of them for a better understanding which will eventually lead to better strategic storytelling.

Strategic storytelling takes place when we EMPATHIZE with our audience. As a result, we understand their WORLDVIEWS which enables us to create RESONANCE with our storytelling efforts. And resonance builds the CONNECTION and moves people into taking action.

Empathy and Storytelling

Empathy (a doing thing)

Empathy can be simply defined as the ability to understand and share the feelings of another person. Let's try to understand this word in the corporate context, where the practice of empathy is gaining momentum (in theory at least). For example, in his book *Hit Refresh*, Microsoft CEO Satya Nadella says his highest priority is to renew his company culture with "a growing sense of empathy." The word *empathy* appears 53 times in the book, but Nadella admits he didn't always have the empathy he does today. However, much like many other concepts such as kindness, generosity, and gratitude, the concept of empathy remains just that for the majority of corporate professionals. Mostly, we understand it as being "nice," not an effort to try to understand and share in others' feelings. This could be because time-poor corporate people find it much easier being nice than exercising real empathy.

Let's try to understand empathy using an element the corporate world is obsessed with—data.

In a recent interaction I had with a product team of a large social media company, I asked a product manager to explain to me what they do. The product manager was creative in the way he responded. He told me to look at one of the social media apps on my phone, then asked, "What do you see?" I said, "I see stuff about running, my friends' photos, and other stuff." He then said, "Aren't those the things you like? See, I understand you."

I took a deep breath and explained to him that, while he might be able to gain knowledge about me based on my platform interactions, he didn't know *why* I like what I like. Therefore, he didn't understand my interests or me. What he thinks of as *understanding* is merely just data about me.

If your company's goal is to forge a connection with customers through communication, you must understand your target market. To understand them, you must demonstrate empathy toward them and become obsessively curious about them. So, empathy in a way is being curious about others. It is the act of wanting to understand others. It's the first step toward strategic storytelling.

Worldviews and Storytelling

What are worldviews? (an understanding thing)

A worldview is a collection of attitudes, values, stories, and expectations about the world around us. Our worldview informs our every thought and action. Or, put simply, it is the story we tell ourselves. It is not necessarily the truth about the world but simply our beliefs about it.

For example, a director shares an insight, and the CEO congratulates him on coming up with and sharing this amazing thought. However, 15 minutes earlier a female junior executive had shared the same insight but was ignored by everyone. Why? It's the bias, the worldview, that the director always has something good to say, and the junior and a female executive, because she is junior, has nothing good to say. Our worldview is a cumulation of all your life experiences. We all have biases, which is part of being human.

Based on our worldviews and biases we tell ourselves a story which is stronger (in our head, at least) than any other story. For example, a friend shared the other day that she was flying from Bangalore, India, to

Singapore and she had noticed that the pilot was a woman. After that discovery, every time there was turbulence she felt very uncomfortable and kept questioning the credibility of the female pilot even though she was aware that she was being biased. Her worldview was so colored by gender expectations that she couldn't help but feel afraid every time the ride got bumpy. The story we tell ourselves will always be the dominant one. Our worldview is a permanently lasered lens on our retina through which we view the world.

When strategic storytelling to our corporate audience, we must ask ourselves questions to understand their worldview:

What keeps them awake at night?

What do they value?

What do they fear?

What motivates them to act?

Where are they unwilling to compromise?

What else don't you know about them?

If you are empathetic, you will see their worldview clearly.

Resonance and Storytelling

Resonance (something we build)

When something resonates, it is because we have said something that reminds someone of something. We know we have built resonance when we elicit responses like these from people:

"That is exactly what happens to me."

"Oh, that's so true."

"That's the story of my life!"

When we frame a story keeping our audience's worldview in mind, we build resonance. For example (referring to Chapter 1), I have built a knowledge bank to help my boss answer all the questions in a shareholder meeting, and I tell the story of the knowledge bank thus:

"Over the last few months, we faced a lot of embarrassment when we were asked for data supporting our strategy, but we didn't have the information. Now there's so much data we have no idea what they will ask, and when they do and we don't know the answers, we feel embarrassed. Moving forward, we'll always have access to this knowledge bank, and it will give us the data point we want at a click of a button."

Now, because you have reminded the boss of a moment when they felt embarrassed, you have built resonance. Good storytelling is not about changing a person's worldview. Instead, it's about framing your story with a very clear understanding of their preexisting worldview. In the process, you find the thread that influences or inspires them to take the desired action.

When we empathize, we understand others' worldviews; when we understand others' worldviews, we build resonance. And when resonance is built, connection takes place.

Connection and Storytelling

Connection (something we create)

In *Gifts of Imperfection*, Dr. Brené Brown describes connection as the energy existing between people when they feel seen, heard, and valued (I've covered this in earlier chapters). Resonance is the key to unlocking connection in communication.

When a meaningful connection is built, trust is built, and action is taken.

Finally, when we empathize, we understand others' worldviews. When we understand others' worldviews, we build resonance. When we build resonance, we create connection. When we create connection, it leads to an action.

In this way, telling strategic stories moves people into a desired direction. As a result, we drive our own success, too.

So far, we've learned *who* storytelling is for. Now it's well and truly time for you to learn *how* to tell strategic stories.

I pledge to remember and apply the following lessons:

- Understanding the storytelling vocabulary helps us build better strategic stories.
- Empathy is the key and the starting point of strategic storytelling.
- A worldview is a collection of attitudes, values, stories, and expectations about the world around us, informing our every thought and action.

- When something resonates it is because we have said something that reminds someone of something. We know we have built resonance when we elicit responses from people.
- Connection is the energy existing between people when they feel seen, heard, and valued.
- Strategic storytelling takes place when we *empathize* with our audience. As a result, we understand their *worldviews*, which enables us to build *resonance* using our storytelling. And resonance creates *connection* and moves people into action.

A Summary of What We've Covered So Far

In Part I of this book, we've learned how adopting the identity of a marketer storyteller teaches us the importance of connection, which is fundamental to strategic storytelling. We learned the following:

- Correct messages alone don't connect.
- Understanding connection is a complex process, and it takes more than one lesson to get it right.
- We can understand the context of connection if we understand the who, why, and how.
- There is a difference between influence and inspiration, and for the corporate boardroom influence is a better fit.
- There are two types of stories, maximal and minimal. Maximal stories are rich in detail and emotion and drive outcomes or generate an action by making people feel, while minimal stories generate action by making people think about the outcomes that can help them be successful.
- The stories that influence management more effectively are those that make a TIM proposition: time, image (i.e. reputation), and money.
- Understanding the vocabulary of storytelling is key: empathy, worldview, resonance, and connection.

Congratulations—that's a whole lot you understand about making a story strategic already!

How to Tell a Strategic Corporate Story

Becoming a reflective, journalist, and reporter storyteller

When I think of this aspect of strategic storytelling, the journalist, author and speaker Malcolm Gladwell comes to mind. I have long admired Malcolm Gladwell's style of storytelling. His writing and speaking are heavily influenced by his background as a journalist. He finds stories and then draws the most nonobvious points from them. His stories are more about the point he is making rather than the characters and what happens to them. I have learned a great deal from his storytelling style and have adapted it to fit the corporate setting. It's a style of storytelling that hasn't been well explored in the corporate world.

Figure 6.1 A reflective, journalist, and reporter storyteller who finds and tells stories to make a change happen

CHAPTER 6

Adopting Corporate Storytelling Identities

THE REFLECTIVE AND JOURNALIST STORYTELLER

● ● ●

Estimated reading time: 10 minutes

Strategic storytelling isn't reserved for leaders only.

In this part of the book, we'll focus on debunking the myth that strategic storytelling is reserved for leaders in organizations only. The truth is, you can be a strategic storyteller from your orientation day, if you adopt the identity of a reflective and journalist storyteller to find stories and then adopt the identity of a reporter to tell those stories effectively.

In 2015, as I was walking out of a boardroom meeting with a few leaders of an organization, I heard one of them say, "If our leaders can be storytellers, we'll achieve great outcomes." I heard this and felt the urge to educate the speaker. I went over to him and asked, "Why only leaders?" His response was: "Because storytelling inspires, and inspiring teams is the job of a leader. And we sure do need some inspirational leaders in our organization at the moment."

This belief is the reason there are so many books, talks, and articles on leadership storytelling. This belief is correct, but incomplete. When storytelling first entered the corporate world there was a huge focus on how leaders could become better storytellers. Steve Denning, one of my favorite authors in the genre of corporate storytelling, wrote a book on the subject in 2007, *The Secret Language of Leadership: How Leaders Inspire Action through Narrative*, which focused on building narratives that visionary leaders can tell to make a change happen.

However, limiting storytelling to leadership is denying it its full potential. The ability to make a change happen using stories extends beyond leadership. The advocacy on storytelling in the corporate world is imbalanced, with too much for leaders and very little for those who will become leaders. Storytelling inspires but can also influence, as we have explored in previous chapters. And your ability to influence shapes your career and the outcomes you can drive from the day you sit in your orientation.

The Changing Identities of the Corporate Storyteller

All corporate professionals can use storytelling, but how you use it at various stages of your career differs. The corporate storytelling ecosystem has identities beyond the well-known one of the visionary leader.

We'll expand on and understand each identity in turn. We won't cover the marketer storyteller identity here because we covered this in Part I. Just bear in mind that the marketer storyteller's role is building connections.

THE REFLECTIVE STORYTELLER

The reflective storyteller is someone who reflects on their own experiences or the experiences of others around them, in the process spotting moments to be used to make a point in a corporate setting. A reflective person is someone who relies on their personal experience and observations. You can be a reflective storyteller from day one of your work.

Here is how a reflective storyteller from the oil and gas industry could tell the story. For the purpose of telling this story we will call this person Mariam who wants to make a case to her boss to approve budget requests to improve the retail experience of their brand.

She uses her own experience to make a point with the story:

I want to make a point about the retail experience of our gas stations. They need to be enhanced to be fast and easy. Let me elaborate my point with my experience.

I bought a diesel car recently. I researched which is the best diesel available in our country, and I was thrilled when my research led me to our brand.

However, a few weeks later, when I went to the gas station to refuel, I was informed there was no diesel in stock. In fact, you can call our gas stations right now, and you'll find a lot of our stations do not have any diesel in stock.

So, I drove to the next gas station which belonged to our competitor brand. I refueled the car, and as I was driving out, I thought what a seamless experience it had been: I got the diesel and paid for it within a minute, and all without having to think too much.

Now, if I had gone to our gas station and even if they had diesel, I would have had to enter my language choice and then made a payment using a rather cumbersome system. I wouldn't have been able to call it a fast and easy experience.

To ensure I was not just relying on my personal experience alone to form this point of view, I called a friend and asked him where he got his fuel from. He candidly told me his choice was our competitor brand. I asked him why. He said, "I've got a motorbike, and filling a motor bike tank at one of your competitor's stations is a very fast process. I don't even have to get off my bike. But if I go to your gas station, while the refueling takes less than a minute, the payment process takes ten minutes because I have to get off my bike, enter my language selection, and then make the payment. So, give me one reason why I should use your brand and not your competitor's? Time is money for me."

After reflecting on my own experience and that of my friend, I gathered data to form an informed point of view. I conducted a survey with questions to give us insights on how and why people make their refueling choices. When I analyzed the data gathered, it was clear to me that we lost potential revenue every day because our retail experience isn't as fast or as easy as our competitor's.

This reflective style is simply an ability to take a moment from your personal experience and use it to make a point with a story. Through her storytelling, Mariam simulated the experience of refueling at her company's gas station and that of a competitor. She was clever enough to realize that her point would be strengthened by adding another story (her friend's) as well as survey data. A perfect blend of story and data helped her influence her bosses and make the change happen.

So here are some questions to help you elicit stories through reflection:

- What exactly is the change I want to make?
- When did I experience the problem to which I am providing a solution?
- Where was I?

- What did my last experience of the problem *feel* like?
- What data do I have to support my story?

There are two key things about the questions here. You need to:

- be clear about the change you are seeking to make.
- identify the feelings associated with the problem you are trying to solve. In my experience, you get to an answer faster when you ask feeling-based questions. Our memory works better when moments are felt.

THE JOURNALIST STORYTELLER

In October 2021, I wrote an article for Forbes Business Council where I wanted to make the point that "data without empathy is empty." For this article, I wanted more than my own experience to make my point. I did my research and came across a story that made the case for why having empathy for your target audience is important. The story was reported in *Inc.* magazine and was about a company active in building and managing a community for a personal care brand. To gain insights into products made by the personal care brand, they formed a community of users and had regular curiosity-filled conversations with them to understand the experience of using their products. In this particular case, the product under discussion was adult diapers.

The goal of this community was to create an environment where people could safely share their thoughts and experiences in relation to the product. One day, a member of this community challenged the community's facilitators to wear adult diapers for a day to help them "fully empathize with what it's like living with incontinence." The team agreed, and the experience was described as "eye-opening," as it helped the brand fully understand its audience's needs.

After I found this example, I also talked to friends whose family members have used this product. What I learned was that most brands focus on things like the material, absorbency, odor, and elasticity of the product, but they don't focus on how it *feels* to wear an adult diaper. It becomes obvious to people you are wearing one after a certain point. This is not something product makers think about. The point is less about the utility of the product but more about the *feelings* associated with it.

In this instance, you can see how I adopted a journalist's identity when storytelling. This identity demands we read, research, and have conversations to find stories beyond our own experience. This requires you to go "into the trenches," just like the journalist does. ("Trenches" in the corporate sphere might mean the places where the corporate culture lives: factory floors, call centers, cafeterias and so on. The places where real conversations take place.) These stories are rich in insights and can challenge and change your existing ways of thinking.

A Good Storyteller Is Also a Good Listener

A good storyteller is a good listener who finds stories to pass on. To find your stories, I recommend you conduct a *story-mining* exercise. In this exercise, you ask people to share examples and moments that reveal and elaborate on their experiences regarding a certain topic.

For example, a couple of years ago, I ran a story-led project where we collected stories from both men and women in a company to understand in what ways exactly women employees were not feeling supported. The data collected from their stories pointed us toward communication being one of the key issues. By exploring the employees' stories, I started to unravel the vexing mystery behind communication.

It was fascinating to learn what the stories revealed. One female team member told a story about a time when her all-male team went out for dinner and did not include her. A male member of the same team told a story about a time when he feared inviting the female team member out to dinner, because she was the only woman and, if he invited her, he worried she would feel uncomfortable. I'll never forget the face of the male team member when he shared his frustration and said, "There is so much education on molestation and harassment in the company, I don't want to invite the female team member and be told that I have done something wrong."

The identity of the journalist storyteller often takes you to places you don't yourself foresee.

QUESTIONS TO HELP YOU ELICIT STORIES FROM OTHERS IN RELATION TO A SPECIFIC TOPIC

- "Share with me a moment when ..."
- "Give me an example ..."

- "What happened?"
- "How did it feel? Take me through it."
- "Where were you when you faced this issue?"
- "Tell me more." (This is a second-layer question, often asked when you get some response but not really a story.)
- Describe the incident from start to finish.

In summary, finding a story is about two things:

- reflecting on your own experiences and observing experiences of others you know
- being a journalist—that is, story-mining through research, reading, surfing the net, or having conversations that take you in new directions.

Now that we have learned how to *find* a story, I need to warn you about the dark space corporate professionals may find themselves in when finding stories to tell. We'll visit this dark space in the next chapter, but only after we make our pledge for this one.

I pledge to remember and apply the following lessons:

- The visionary leader is not the only storyteller identity.
- A strategic corporate storyteller has multiple storytelling identities they can adopt: a reflective, journalist, reporter, and marketer storyteller.
- A reflective storyteller reflects on their own experiences and observes the experiences of those around them to find a moment and use that moment to make a point.
- A journalist storyteller finds stories by reading, researching, surfing the net, and conducting story-mining exercises.
- In the process of finding and telling a story, you don't just adopt one identity but many identities along the way.

Let's now learn about the dark space corporate professionals can find themselves in while looking for a story. Hint: It's the kind of stories they are looking for.

CHAPTER 7

The Dark Space of Corporate Storytelling

● ● ●

Estimated reading time: 3 minutes

Big stories can be a dark space.

When I was running a large change story project in a factory, this is what a factory safety officer shared with me:

"Anjali, our incident report is filled with information about the minor accidents that happen every day. People only pay attention to big accidents. As a result, minor accidents occur frequently. It's the low-consequence nature of minor accidents that prevents people from paying attention to them. But, put together, these minor accidents create high consequences. And it's only when we learn to understand the value of compounded incremental gains from fixing these small issues that we can make a big change happen."

A similar truth comes into play with the kinds of stories people use in the corporate setting. Mostly, people look for stories where there's a large element of the unexpected or surprise. Take, for example, the story of Chesley ("Sully") Sullenberger, a now-retired US airline pilot best known for his heroism as captain of US Airways Flight 1549 when he landed the plane in the Hudson River in 2009 after both engines were disabled by a bird strike. All 155 people aboard survived. His story is interesting because the chances of a plane being able to land success-fully and without casualties in a river seem remote. But stories with this kind of unexpected element are rare in the corporate setting. The key problem with this kind of story, though, is not so much that we don't have enough of them to tell but that they don't really change day-to-day behaviors on the ground because they appear too farfetched. They are highly engaging, especially when you first listen to them, but they are not able to make a change happen. Their high engagement value doesn't translate into high potential to make change happen. They are just too heroic for the corporate setting!

In a Corporate Setting, It's the Small Stories That Can Make Change Happen

In the corporate setting, we give priority to the stories that can make a change happen, not to stories that are entertaining or unusual.

For example, here's a story first published in *The Washington Post*: Upon President Obama's inauguration, the large majority of his top aides were men, which led to complaints from women about their exclusion from significant meetings and their opinions being disregarded when they did participate. To combat this, female staffers adopted a technique known as "amplification," in which they would reiterate important points made by their female colleagues during meetings and explicitly give them credit for their ideas. This strategy aimed to compel the male attendees to acknowledge and appreciate the contributions of their female counterparts while preventing them from taking credit for the women's ideas.

Now this story, although it comes from perhaps the most influential boardroom on the planet, is a story that resonates with many women. It is certainly not farfetched; it's the story of many women working in corporations. For this reason, the story has the power to make change happen.

As a reflective and journalist storyteller in a corporate setting, you should look for stories that are low on the surprise or rarity factor because it is in the compounded incremental changes of small stories that a large change happens. Also, these stories resonate: They remind people of their own experiences. Remember, it's your overall identity to be a successful changemaker, not a teller of surprising stories!

In the next chapter, we'll learn how to be a reporter storyteller, but before that let's take this chapter's pledge.

I pledge to remember and apply the following lessons:

- I don't have to look for stories with big, unexpected events to be a changemaker.
- Stories with small unexpected events have the power to make me a successful changemaker.

CHAPTER 8

Becoming a Reporter Storyteller

STRUCTURING AND TELLING STORIES

● ● ●

Estimated reading time: 14 minutes

You may have found a story to tell, but that doesn't guarantee you can structure it and tell it well.

The Difference Between a Journalist and a Reporter

Before we dig deeper into this chapter, we need to understand the difference between a journalist and a reporter. These terms are often used interchangeably, but there's a crucial distinction. If you are to adopt the right storytelling identity, you need to understand the difference.

The main difference between a journalist and a reporter is that, while the journalist's job is to research new stories, the reporter's job is to relay that story to the public. Journalists work for newspapers, magazines, and other written platforms. Reporters report the news on television, radio, or any other mass media. Now that's clear, let's return to our corporate professional who dons various identities to make a change happen via strategic storytelling.

Oral Storytelling Skill Takes Precedence over Written Storytelling Skills

As a corporate professional, your ability to shape and tell an oral story well matters a lot more than your ability to write a story well. It is rare to come across a corporate professional who has been given negative feedback on their ability to write a story, whereas ineffectiveness while orally telling a story in the boardroom often draws comment. The point is that, for the corporate professional, the skill to structure and tell an oral story is far more valuable than the skill to write a story.

However, there is a barrier you will face when oral storytelling despite your burning desire to tell the story. Vanessa's story uncovers the barrier for us.

Vanessa, one of my clients and a corporate professional, attended one of my talks on strategic storytelling at a conference in Sydney. Soon after the talk she connected with me on my social channels and sent me a message via LinkedIn. Her message read: "Thank you. I learned so much. I can't wait to tell strategic stories." Two years later, I bumped into Vanessa at another conference and asked her how she was getting along with storytelling. Her response was disheartening but telling: "Even though I wanted to tell a story, I struggled to find opportunities, and even when I did, I failed to structure and tell the story well." How had this come about?

My keynote in Sydney which Vanessa had attended was designed to inspire my audiences to *think* about the profound difference between storytelling and strategic storytelling, not to *teach* them how to shift their storytelling into strategic storytelling. The focus of the keynote was to make my audience think differently about the way they position their storytelling efforts to the target audience. Vanessa's inability to find opportunities to tell stories and her struggle with structuring and telling the story even when an opportunity did come up is a common challenge faced by corporate professionals.

The two problems—lack of opportunity and inability to structure— are linked: If you don't know how to *structure* a story, you will never know where to *place* a story. Knowing how to structure a story not only makes you see stories that you would normally not even identify as stories, but also makes you see opportunities to tell a story well. Finding a story is all well and good but structuring and telling it well is great. No matter how good the story is, it's not doing its job if it's not told well.

The Secret Is in the Structuring and Telling

Knowing what makes a strategic story and being able to find it is not enough; you must learn how to structure and tell your strategic story. Vanessa's example throws light on two issues you will run into:

1. **Your story opportunities are invisible.** Opportunities to tell stories may not be obvious. You must know your story's structure to be able to find where it fits. In the absence of a story structure, you might default to standard corporate speak. You may find yourself looking at your PowerPoint presentation and thinking there's no opportunity to tell a story here. Most of the time, though, corporate presentations do have room for a story.

2. **More crucially, even if you have a story, you need to work on telling it well.** One of my favorite commercials bringing this point to life was made by Nokia. In the commercial, you see two couples sitting in a garden catching up. I will call them Couple 1 (the couple who didn't go on holiday) and Couple 2 (the couple who did). This is how the conversation flows between them:
   Couple 1: So glad you could make it. How was the safari?
   Couple 2: It was amazing.
   Couple 1: So, tell us more. Did you see animals?
   Couple 2: Oh, so many animals, so many animals.
   Couple 1: Well, tell us more. Was it magical?
   Couple 2 (wife): (looking at the husband) Tell them about …
   Couple 2 (husband): It was an animal that could have taken your head off.
   Couple 2 (wife): But it was sweet.
   Couple 2 (husband): But man-eating.
   Couple 2 (wife): But what was it?

Couple 2 is trying hard to tell the story of the safari but just doesn't know how to. And the frame cuts to the voiceover:

You are a storyteller, just not a good one.

Being able to tell a story well needs more than having a story to tell. You need to learn how to structure your story.

Story Structures

A lot of us understand the value of storytelling. We have stories to tell but never tell them because we do not know how exactly to structure them in our time-poor corporate world. In other words, you may well have done your work as a reflective storyteller and a journalist storyteller and have your story to hand, but this doesn't guarantee you will be able to tell a story *like a reporter*. Telling a story in a compelling manner is about communication skills.

In his book *Building a Story Brand: Clarify Your Message So Customers Will Listen*, Donald Miller explains the importance of becoming a reporter using the idea of noise versus notes. Both are made up of the same thing—traveling sound waves. However, one is annoying, and the other is pleasant. It's about the way they are organized. In music, the composer takes everything extraneous out and arranges the sound waves to achieve the effect they want. Being a reflective and journalist storyteller allows you to find a story, but if you do not organize it well like a reporter you run the risk of turning your story into noise.

Let's learn how to structure storytelling strategically for a time-poor corporate audience. As we saw in Chapter 4, there are two types of structure you need to learn to report stories well in the corporate world—maximal and minimal—each tuned to a different audience. The maximal story, with its emphasis on emotion and detail, is for employees, while the minimal story, focused on outcomes, is for the senior leadership team. And corresponding to each story type is a process through which you, the strategic storyteller, need to go. In this chapter, we'll address the maximal story process. The minimal story process will be the focus of Chapter 11.

The Maximal Story: A Story for Employees

Figure 8.1 The maximal story

As we have seen, the maximal story is rich in details. It acknowledges that the audience wants to hear the full story so they can connect with it. There are four steps to the story process, and you will see how through the process you adopt different identities (see the left-hand side in Figure 8.1). We will cover Steps 1 to 3 in this chapter and Step 4 in Chapter 9 (the next chapter).

STEP 1: THE MARKETER STORYTELLER: WHAT'S THE KEY MESSAGE YOU WANT TO CONVEY?

This could be clear statements such as:

- "We have to rebalance our food product portfolio so it's more about health than fun."
- "Cloud migration can be made easy with proper planning."

When I work with corporate professionals, I often notice they lack clarity on what exactly is the key message they want to convey. They have a vague idea, but clarity is yet to be achieved. In such situations, it's important to spend as much time as required to gain clarity on the key message. Usually, if you keep asking what exactly the key message is, you eventually land on the right one. It's an iterative process.

For example, I recently worked with a senior auditor who said, "I want to build a story to sell our auditing services. That's my key message." The story she told to support the key message was:

In 2019, we had just won an audit service. Previously, the company was audited by X, a Big Four public accounting firm. Company X had been their incumbent for ten years, so it was a tough fight for us. I want to share how we won.

We submitted the proposal and then were given an opportunity to have a discussion. During the discussion, the client mentioned our fees and said, "That's three times more than the incumbent's fees. How can you justify that?"

We explained to them that our fees represented value for money because we would provide not only an audit report but also training for their staff that would keep them abreast of ever-changing industry standards. "We don't just provide audit services," we told them, "we take responsibility for your success." During the first meeting, we highlighted to them some obvious errors they were making and how they could prove risky in the near future.

Now, if you look at this story, the key message of the story is not selling auditing services but providing value for money. This is a smart key message because often when we articulate a key message we end up focusing on the outcome we want rather than the outcome the people we seek to serve want. Your desired outcome may be selling your services, but it shouldn't be the key message that is communicated. The story the auditor told in this case was brilliant because it was hyper-focused on making the client successful.

The other issue with key messages is that corporate professionals tend to make them overly tactical. For example, here is how a story's key message was articulated for the launch of a cloud migration webinar: "Announcing the launch of the cloud migration webinar."

This is clearly a *tactical* key message: It informs the audience about the tactic or, put simply, what the corporate professional is doing. Tactical key messages do not address the "why" of the webinar. As a result, they fail to connect emotionally with the person the webinar is intended to serve.

So we might amend the message thus:

You can strip away the stress associated with cloud migration. Join us for a webinar and learn how.

By changing the key message, we've done the following:

- We've empowered the reader by adding "you." This gives the reader the power to take an action and make a change happen.

- We've acknowledged that stress is a primary emotion associated with cloud migration. So by bringing the audience's emotional state into the message, we have created resonance.

Tactical key messages don't connect. Period. Key messages with the power to connect are the ones that address the emotional state of the audience, create resonance, and influence them to make a change happen.

Activity: Getting your key message right

In my strategic storytelling sessions, I often get my clients to do this exercise to sharpen their key messages:

Imagine walking into the room where you are going to tell a story to your intended audience. What is your opening line? This will be your key message. Think in particular about why it should matter to the people listening to you.

Key messages should not be confused with your desired outcome. It is a message designed for the audience.

Below is a structured approach to designing your key message. The key message is the first line you say to your audience before you tell the actual story.

1. Start with how long you are going to speak for. Remember we are in a time-poor corporate world. Omit this step where not necessary. For example: *In the next 15 minutes...*

2. What is the main point you want to make? This point has to keep your audience in mind.
   For example, "Will it help us regain the number one position in the market?"
   So, combining our first two points here: *In the next 15 minutes, I want to share how we can regain the number one position in the market.*

3. How are you proposing that the goal will be reached? For example, it might be by acquiring new analytics software.

Now I will combine 1, 2, and 3: *In the next 15 minutes, I want to share how we can regain the number one position by acquiring new analytics software.*

Then, at the end of your story, add what you want the audience to do. In this example, we want them to try out a free trial, so combining 1, 2, 3, and 4, we have: *In the next 15 minutes, I want to share how we can regain the number one position by acquiring the new analytics software, and my request is for you to consider the free trial as our next step.*

Here are some acronyms I have developed to help my clients structure the opening line for an effective delivery of the story:

TPRA for situations where you need to influence.

TPIA for situations where you need to inspire.

Where:

T stands for the **time** you will take to present.

P stands for the **point** you want to make.

R stands for the **results** you want to get (your results mostly will fall under time, image/reputation, save/make money).

I stands for **identity**. In inspiring situations, you would replace **R**—results—with **I**—**identity**—what your listeners will end up becoming because they have embraced the proposed change (for example, Green Activist, Data Driven, Workforce of the Future, etc.).

A stands for **action**, the action you would like your audience to take.

The key message, set out in the first line of your presentation, sets you up for success. This way of structuring your first line achieves the following outcomes:

- It puts your time-poor corporate audience at ease because you are showing that you respect their time (they know straightaway why they are here).
- It helps them understand *why* they should listen to you.
- It clearly establishes what will enable their success.
- It makes it clear to them what you want them to do when you are done.

When I first started working with corporate professionals, I used to think my role was to work on stories with them. But, a decade later, I've realized that my role is to help them to uncover their key message, find the story, curate the story, and then help them tell the story well. Getting clarity on key messages is not as simple as it sounds. It requires deep thinking if you want your message to connect with the people you wish to change.

STEP 2: THE REFLECTIVE AND JOURNALIST STORYTELLER: WHAT IS THE STORY I CAN TELL TO CONVEY THE MESSAGE?

This step is all about your ability to find a story from your experiences or any other source. Here we are asking you to be a reflective and journalist storyteller (see Chapter 6 if you need to revise this).

STEP 3: THE MARKETER STORYTELLER: DOES THIS STORY RESONATE WITH YOUR AUDIENCE?

Now, you may have the story but, if it doesn't resonate, it will not drive the desired outcome. We covered this in detail in Part I of this book. Who is your story for? Reminder, the identity we are asking you to adopt here is of a marketer who makes sure their story is sticky because it connects. You want to get your audience to a place where they can say, "Oh that's so true!", meaning not so much that your story is factually true (though of course that matters) but that it resonates.

STEP 4: THE REPORTER STORYTELLER: IT IS TIME TO ASSEMBLE THE STORY FOR EFFECTIVE TELLING.

This will be the topic for our next chapter, but before we get to this, we need to take this chapter's pledge.

I pledge to remember and apply the following lessons:

- Becoming a reporter means you can tell your story in a compelling way.
- There are two types of stories every corporate should learn to tell: maximal and minimal.
- Maximal stories are rich in detail and acknowledge that the audience wants to listen to the full story so that it resonates with them.
- There are four key steps to telling a story:
  - Step 1 is about being a marketer storyteller and structuring the key message in such a way that it connects.

- o Step 2 is about being a reflective and journalist storyteller and finding the story you can tell.
- o Step 3 is again about being a marketer storyteller and ensuring the story resonates.
- o Step 4 is about assembling the story.

So let's now turn to how you can *assemble* a maximal story. We'll keep how you can turn your maximal story into a minimal one for another chapter.

CHAPTER 9

Assembling a Maximal Story

PART 1

● ● ●

Estimated reading time: 13 minutes

The spontaneity of stories is mostly a fallacy.

Earlier this year I was invited to be a part of a conversation where I found myself in between storytelling practitioners from various industries. There were scriptwriters, novelists, someone from TED Talks, and even a NASA Chief Story Architect. To be honest, I felt a bit overwhelmed—not because I felt intimidated by their titles or brands but because the storytelling principles they were discussing were so profound that I struggled to find a fit for them in the corporate world.

One of the discussions, for example, was about building complex characters. Now if you've worked for a corporation, you'll know our world is complex enough without setting ourselves the task of creating characters for our stories! But that doesn't mean we can't use stories; only that corporate stories require a different style and approach from, say, fictional ones. So, in this chapter, I want to decode those styles so you can create stories that drive your success.

There are seven elements in assembling a maximal story, but it is important to take note that the elements are a guide, not a rule-book, to building stories. The idea is to help very busy corporate professionals put stories to work and make a change happen efficiently. If you would like to read other books on this topic, the inspiration for these seven elements is the story-spotting framework in Shawn Callahan's book *Putting Stories to Work: Mastering Business Storytelling.* There are some similarities between Shawn's Story Spotting framework

Figure 9.1 The maximal story

and my Maximal Story framework but overall it differs. It helps a very busy corporate professional put stories to work and make a change happen efficiently.

Now let's look at them one by one. Figure 9.1, which we've already encountered in Chapter 8, provides an overview.

1. Calendar Marker, Time Marker and Place Marker

Recently a client of mine shared this story with his team members to help build a more inclusive culture in the company

Mumbai, January 22, 1992, at around 3 p.m. I received my test results that indicated that I had been diagnosed with a serious illness. My doctor said, "You need six months off of work to recover."

At that time, my job was assistant manager in a factory and I had ten team members including some young engineers. I carried out almost all the major jobs myself. My team was young, and I didn't really trust their ability to get the job done.

76

I needed to hand over to a senior engineer in a day and I found it very tough. But I had no choice because I was to be hospitalized the very next day. The senior engineer who I had to hand over to was already overworked. I struggled to figure out how to hand over everything smoothly to him.

One of my major jobs was rather complicated if you lacked experience. I decided to hand over this job to one of the younger engineers. I wasn't sure if he could do the job.

After I left, the young engineer went to the factory every day and collected data with the senior engineer's support. He achieved the target after three months, thus reducing the workload of the senior engineer.

After six months, I had recovered and I came back to my previous job and recognized that all my team members had improved immensely. I had left them inexperienced, but now they knew their jobs very well. My absence had accelerated the young engineers' learning. Each team member now had the ability to execute major jobs in their role, which had not been the case before I left.

After this experience I realized that I had been a roadblock in the young engineers' growth. I could easily have included them in my workload earlier but my biases had acted as a roadblock.

Notice how the story starts, with a very clear day of the week, time of day, and place. This is a common practice in news articles, where getting the facts straight at the outset is crucial. If you use the same style in your corporate stories, you immediately avoid the risk of your audience perceiving you as a fictional storyteller, who, of course, has a very different purpose. You are setting your story firmly in the factual world.

Here are some ways you can start:

- Time markers are usually more general references to time such as "just the other day," "last week," or "five years ago."

- Calendar markers are more specific than time markers and give the precise month or even day, for example "In August 2020 …" or "On September 5, 2017 …".

- Place markers are real-world cities or countries you might spot on a map: Los Angeles, Singapore, Thailand, and so on. If your audience is likely to be familiar with the location, you can make things more specific. If you are speaking to an audience from Singapore, for example, you'll be able to mention Tan Tock Seng Hospital without worrying too much that your audience won't know the location.

These markers make sure that the audience understands that the story is factual from the outset. They will help you overcome the entrenched view that stories are made up and meant only for entertainment. They are a smart way to start a story because they set you up as someone who is here to tell the truth like a reporter.

One of my biggest observations about using markers like this has been that it changes the way people view you. If you start off by saying, "I am going to tell you a story," people perceive you as an entertainer. However, if you start off by saying, "I want to share what happened in one of our banks in the UK in January 2020," people perceive you as someone who is telling the truth. They may not call you a storyteller, but they will most definitely call you an effective and credible communicator who can make a change happen. This is exactly the goal of strategic storytelling.

2. Setting That Activates Visualization

Dr. John Medina, through his newsletter *Brain Rules*, has taught us that vision trumps all the other senses. One of the most common mistakes corporate communicators make is to not activate their audience's visualization through their communication. This is not because they don't want to; it's just that they don't know how to. One simple way to activate visualization is by using statements like these:

- "I was in a meeting room …"
- "We started the Zoom meeting and within five minutes we had 25 people on the call."
- "I walked into the boardroom and my boss was already there."

What's common to all these statements is that they take you into space (even if's just a digital space): A meeting room, a Zoom meeting, a boardroom … Your audience knows what these spaces look like, and they instantly form a picture of them inside their head. You have activated your audience's visualization.

It's worth remembering at this point that we think and feel in images and not in words. For example, if I say the word "garden," do you see a garden, or do you see the letters that make up the word? This is a no-brainer: We see a garden and not the alphabet. *This is because we think and feel in images, and not in words.* This is why visualization is so important: It enables us to think clearly.

Here is another corporate example where you can see how to activate visualization. This example concerns a client of mine at the peak of COVID-19 pandemic. The company that used this story originated in India but now has presence in more than 25 countries. The reason I mention the country is because, as you will see, some Asian values are at play here.

First, a bit of context.

As a leader, you've noted how morale is sinking in your organization due to factors beyond your control. The wellbeing of your employees has always been your top priority, no matter what the situation, so, to boost morale, you decide to remind people how they have been cared for all these years and how the company will continue to care for them. To achieve this, you produce a video of yourself reiterating this message, and this is how your script begins:

Since the inception of our company, employee care has been our top priority. We have in place an effective process that takes care of you and your family's needs, too, in difficult times.

This line is only an assertion of a fact or belief, and a missed opportunity to communicate effectively. While you as a teller may know there's conviction in your statement, the listener will miss the point because it sounds too much like just one of those corporate statements trotted out time and time again.

There's a simple solution at hand to make this a story that appeals to your audience's capacity for visualization and thus their emotions:

Since the inception of our company, employee care has been our top priority. We have an effective process which takes care of you and your family's needs. Do you remember your first day with the company when the CEO came to see you at the orientation? You were all seated on level 7 of the building with your orientation packs, and you were given benefits including grants for education overseas, insurance coverage, and a welcome pack with an employees' handbook and movie tickets for the family.

(Now to some of you this may seem patronizing, but I just want to remind you that the origin of this company lies in India and it is not uncommon for companies in Asia to welcome not just the employee but also the families to the organization through small gestures like movie tickets.)

Can you feel the difference between the first and second narration? In the second narration, the viewers can visualize the story. They are

79

transported back to their first day with the company. They are not just listening to an assertion of fact but are connecting to a story because it is building resonance.

A good way to activate visualization is through the use of *schemas*. Schema is a technical term used by psychologists, but for our purposes I want you to simply remember it as layers of memory built into our sub-conscious. For example, when I say the word *Paris*, one of the following images will likely pop up in your head:

- the Eiffel Tower
- a croissant
- a big museum like the Louvre.

A lot of the time what comes into your mind is based on the memory in your head built on the experiences you have had. That is the *schema* you have for Paris.

In a corporate setting, using schemas to engage is a great strategy. If you talk about a place that your audience have a schema for, you activate their visualization and their brains take them to the place in your story—a factory, a plant, a meeting room, a boardroom, and so on. Activation of visualization is an important tool for the strategic storyteller, although it should be used subtly—with the intention not to entertain but to make a change happen.

3. People Having a Dialogue

Stories are about people, and people must have names. Let's begin with people.

Read the following two paragraphs and ask yourself which is more likely to tug at your heartstrings (the situation and people described here are of course entirely fictional):

- *Last week in XX country, a bridge collapsed while close to 80 workers were carrying out maintenance work either on or under the bridge. All the workers died. We have set up a fundraiser to support the families of the deceased. If you would like to contribute, please go to: www.XXXX*

- *It was a normal working day for Mohan Talpadia, a 42-year-old construction worker and the father of three children, all under ten years old.*

He came to the bridge close to National Highway XX to carry out his maintenance duties to earn a daily wage equivalent to two US dollars, but sometime around midday there was a loud noise of concrete crumbling and people screaming. Mohan, along with 80 other workers, died on the spot. The families of the workers depended on the daily wage these men earned, and now they need your support. To help Mohan's family and other workers' families, please contribute here: www.XXXX

Most people will choose 2 because there is an *identifiable character*, in this case Mohan. These findings are from research conducted by Deborah Small, a Wharton marketing professor, and her colleagues. Please take note that the term originally used by Professor Small was *identifiable victim*, but we have changed this here to suit the smaller stories we use in the corporate setting. Mostly we are dealing not with victims but only with characters in corporate settings.

Approach 2 connects with us because it has people. People contribute because they want to make a difference. If they are unable to see themselves making a difference because their contribution is like a drop in the ocean, they would rather not do it.

For this reason, when we want our busy corporate people to take time out of their day-to-day work and do something, a story about a particular business development manager named, say "Maria," is far better than story about business development managers in general. Saying "Maria, who is a business development manager for an IT firm, was finding it hard to work with increasing client demands" is better than saying "Business development managers of IT firms are challenged by increasing client demands," because the manager may be able to do something about Maria because she is an identifiable character.

Hearing a name leads us to believe we can make a difference to an existing problem, where otherwise the problem may appear too generic or hard to solve. When it comes to our hearts, a single human story trumps the report about the many.

So, if you get asked, "What's in a name?" your answer should be: A name can inspire a desired action. The characters often have a dialogue which makes the story come to life.

As a side note, in *The Leader's Guide to Storytelling: Mastering the Art and Discipline of Business Narrative*, Stephen Denning points out that it is good practice not to have more than two characters in an oral story.

This is simply because having lots of characters can confuse the audience and it's not long before they're wondering who's saying what to whom.

At the start of this book, I promised to keep the chapters short. We have so far covered three of the elements of the maximal story. In the next chapter, we'll look at the remaining four elements, but first we need to make our pledge.

I pledge to remember and apply the following lessons:

- The maximal story has seven elements, three of which are:
  1 Using time markers, calendar markers, and place markers helps you position yourself as someone who is telling the truth, much like a reporter.
  2 Activating visualization is a good strategy because we think and feel in images. Leveraging schemas is a good way to activate visualization.
  3 Stories have people, and people have names.

Now let's move on to the rest of the elements.

CHAPTER 10

Assembling a Maximal Story

● ● ●

Estimated reading time: 13 minutes

Some of us are gifted storytellers, but the rest of us can do an equally good job by following a structured approach.

We have so far covered three elements of the maximal story. In this chapter, we will cover the remaining four.

4. Emotion

In June 2011, in San Francisco, Steve Jobs launched iCloud at the Worldwide Developers Conference. At one point in his presentation (which you can watch on YouTube) he talks about the frustration involved in keeping the devices in sync. He describes the frustration by using the words "crazy" and the audience bursts into a spontaneous applause. The word *crazy* clearly resonated with his audience—you can hear and see their emotional response to Jobs's story.

Mentioning emotions in a story does two things:

- It makes your audience feel seen—because you are acknowledging how they feel in a certain situation. It labels an emotion they are feeling.

- It allows the teller to express their own emotional connection with the story and thus provoke a similar emotional connection in the audience. If you say, "I ran a project in China and the project failed," this conveys a very different feeling than saying, "I ran a project in China, the project failed, and I was devastated." Your audience sees your emotional connection to the project and thus find it easier to develop an emotional connection themselves.

Using emotion in this way is about learning how to *describe* emotions, not about putting your emotions *on display*. I learned this from David Hutchens, the author of *Circle of the 9 Muses: A Storytelling Field Guide for Innovators and Meaning Makers*. In 2015, I asked him a question during a book club session that roughly ran like this: "In the corporate world, the moment you mention emotions are important in stories, you always get eye-rolling and a look that says, "No way am I mixing emotions with work. Emotions and work don't go together. So, how do you manage to inject your soul into dry documents about strategy, process, and policy without getting emotional?"

The answer I got from David was both practical and insightful. Again, I'm paraphrasing: "What we need to understand is that, when we ask corporate leaders to describe emotions, we are not asking them to display emotions. There's a difference between describing and displaying emotions. Describing is giving an account in words. Displaying is a performance, show, or event staged for public entertainment."

So saying something like "I was frustrated with the failure of Project Heartbeat" is very different from showing your frustration by stamping your feet, shaking your first, or raising your voice.

5. Connected Events

A story is simply a connected series of events—things happening one after the other. Stories are often wrapped in phrases like "this happened," "then this happened," and "in the end this happened." In a corporate setting, you might wonder: Have I got the time to narrate a series of events. Will the story become too long for a time-poor corporate audience? And is it even important? Let's answer these questions one by one:

Do I have the time to narrate a series of events? Will the story become too long for a time-poor corporate audience?

The time it takes to tell a story is often dependent on the number of events you use. The greater the number of events, the longer it takes to tell the story, though not every event contributes toward the point you are making with the story. If you are time poor, look at each event and delete the ones that are not contributing toward the point you are making.

Beware: Sometimes we decide to retain an event because we feel attached to it. All I can say is: Delete ruthlessly. Remember, the story you're telling is not for yourself; it's to motivate people into action. Personally, I reduce the number of events to the bare minimum when I'm speaking to management and increase them slightly when I'm speaking to employees.

Is it even important to share a series of events?

Well, if you don't have a series of events, most likely you are just sharing a single example:

Story – Series of events = Example

For example, if I asked you, "Which was the last successful brand campaign you ran?" and you responded by saying, "The XYZ campaign," that would hardly be insightful. An example of a successful campaign answers my question but it's not a story. The problem with such responses is they strip away any potential for creating a connection by using a story.

Examples do a great job of building credibility but are rarely insightful and often lack the ability to make a connection. In the absence of a series of events, you are denying the audience a chance to become invested in the outcome and create a connection.

Let me elaborate by using a story told to me by one of my clients.

In 2015, I had an opportunity to work with the communications team of a multinational engineering and electronics company on brand storytelling. One of the participants told a story that establishes the importance of living company values and not just talking about them. Here is that story:

I was the newly appointed Corporate Communications Manager. During my orientation, I was informed that the company allowed flexi hours and had a work from home policy. When I heard this, I rolled my eyes: How would that be possible? There's always so much to do.

On my second day at work, I had to sit in an external meeting with my boss and it was my first chance to create an impression on him. So, I got myself ready well in time for the morning. It was raining heavily, but I was driving to work so I carried on without thinking too much about the rain. A few minutes later, I found myself in a traffic jam due to the floods the rain had caused.

I was stressed and sweating. I was afraid I would not get to the office for my very first meeting with my boss. I called my boss, and the PA informed me that the meeting had already started. I was devastated. Then, I somehow gathered courage and decided to send a text message to my boss explaining

I was stuck. The response I got back from my boss was: It happens! Turn back and work from home. Remember we are fair."

His behavior to me was a demonstration of values in action. One of our values was fairness, and he was being fair. I developed an instant liking for him and learned a lesson of making sure my behavior was in line with our company values. Values, I realized, are something living and breathing.

Now, just imagine if this person had just said, "Our company practices being fair, and we don't just talk about values but live them. For example, my boss recently allowed me to work from home when it was raining heavily." While the story connects with the reader/listener, the example makes no connection at all.

Every time I ask corporate professionals to replace examples with strategic stories on certain occasions, they churn out the same old answer that they need to stay efficient and productive in a time-poor corporate world and that telling tales just sucks up too much time. I would say the contrary: *not* telling strategic stories sucks up time, and here's why.

In 2016, I attended a talk by the chief storyteller of a large multinational—let's call it corporation ABC. In his talk, he shared a story about how at one stage the ABC team was looking for a certain technology to enhance one of its existing products. The team researched intensively, and after hours of research they finally found someone who had the technology. The team read the paper about the technology excitedly, but when they got to the end of the paper they saw its source—ABC UK. What they had been looking for across the globe was already available within their own world. The whole process, the chief storyteller said, had been a waste of time—and precisely because the people in the organization weren't telling each other stories. If we shift our knowledge in to stories, we will get both high-quality listening and retention.

One of the reason why the story is sticky is because it has a series of events that connect and naturally connect with us. Distilled examples fail to do that.

6. Something Happens

Using the unexpected can prevent a series of events from becoming flat or stale. For example, in the story I shared earlier about making values stick using stories, the response the teller got from her boss was:

"It happens! Turn back and work from home. Remember we are fair." This is unexpected; the teller did not expect this to happen. In fictional or artistic storytelling, we often call this a plot twist, but this term somehow seems inappropriate for a time-poor corporate audience, which isn't listening to be entertained after all. So, here we will stick to something much simpler for the last part of our key message: "Something happens".

Let me elaborate on the unexpected with a story shared by a company auditor with his chief financial officer. The point the auditor wanted to make was: "Accountants should always upgrade their knowledge and stay relevant." This seems like common sense, but just wait till the story ends:

In 2020, we all woke up to the news the accounting standards in our country had changed. After the news, what followed was the heavy burden of having to learn the new standards as soon as possible. Somewhere in the process we realized that we weren't ready, and the learning curve was steeper than we thought. We didn't have the time we thought we did.

To cater to the speed, we engaged external accounting consultants who were equipped with the latest know-how on the new accounting standards. The external accountants did a fantastic job of managing the change in the first year. We all smiled with relief and pride when we managed to close the books for the year. However, then came the year 2021 and our internal accountants started to struggle again. We realized we had made a mistake: There had been no transfer of knowledge to our organization and our own accounting team remained without the new expertise required in this ever-changing environment. Consequently, we needed to engage external consultants again to at least help with the first quarter of the year.

But the point is: How long can we keep on doing this? It is time for us to invest in upgrading our accountants rather than keep getting external help.

If we look at this story, there are a couple of unexpected moments:

- the new accounting standards which are where the story begins
- the fact that, the year after, the company is again in a difficult situation where its own team of accountants still has no clue how to navigate the change.

It is these unexpected events that make the story seem insightful and interesting, rather than just common sense. The point strikes home, motivating action.

Another area in a corporate setting where lack of focus on including the unexpected in a story is the case study. A typical format of a case study is given in Figure 10.1, on the left-hand side.

- This was the problem.
- This was the solution.
- This was the implementation.
- This was the result.

Figure 10.1 The difference between a case study and a success story

Now if you look at the right-hand side of the figure, when we include "why the problem existed" in between "the problem" and "the solution," that gives us insight.

It's not just about articulating a problem and providing a solution but also about understanding why the problem existed: What led to the problem is what makes a story a good one. This becomes the *unexpected* element of the story.

Additionally, if we become specific about whose problem we are solving, then the case study can become a success story. In this case, we are solving Mary's problem. Remember the earlier feature of maximal stories we looked at about stories having people.

7. Reiterating the Key Message

We are now back to where we started, the importance of the key message, which we covered in Chapter 8. You may be wondering why are we back to where we started? That's because the delivery of a story is like a hamburger.

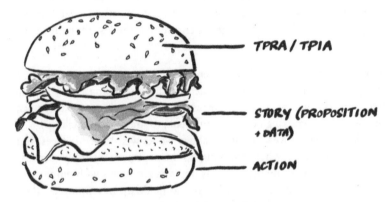

Figure 10.2 The delivery of the story

- **Top:** Start with the key message, the part of the story that akin to the top slice of the bun. Remember the two acronyms we looked at in Chapter 8: TPRA (to influence) or TPIA (to inspire), which are the two ways you can start the story.
- **Middle:** In the middle is the patty or your story, which is the story you want to tell. The story must be accompanied by a proposition and at least one data point that supports the story. Telling a story is not enough, you must have a proposition. I will cover story proposition in detail in Chapter 12.
- **Bottom:** Finally, there is the bottom slice of the bun where we make the same key message we started with, so that the focus is firmly on the action you want people to take.

There are a few reasons why we close with the key message:

- It helps you keep your story on point. When you know how you are going to end your story, you end it just at the right time with the right message. It avoids the story just going on and on, open-ended.

- It reinforces the most important part of a business story which is the key message. In maximal stories, we run the risk of our corporate audiences getting caught up in the characters and emotions and forgetting that, in the end, what we need is an action. Therefore, by closing with the key message we ensure that the last thought in the audience's mind is the key message.

You have now learned the key elements to look out for when assembling a story. However, it is important to remember that assembling a story is not a linear process, and you don't always need to use every element. Remember, the elements serve as a guide, not a rulebook, to strategic storytelling.

The rich story we've outlined above works well for employees, but it sometimes fails when speaking to management—simply because what connects with management is not what connects with employees. Although management, of course, is also made up of employees, their connection levers are different.

In the next chapter, we'll learn how to tell a minimal story, but first we need to make our pledge:

I pledge to remember and apply the following lessons:

- The maximal story has seven elements. We have covered three in the previous chapter, the remaining four are:
  4 Bringing in emotion, by describing (not displaying) emotions
  5 Using connected series of events to bring connection
  6 Using the unexpected to make the story insightful
  7 Reiterating the key message at the end of the story, as this is what matters most to the corporate audience—the focus here should be on the desired action part of the key message.

Now let's learn about assembling a minimal story.

CHAPTER 11

Assembling a Minimal Story

● ● ●

Estimated reading time: 4 minutes

Our success sometimes lies in making things minimal.

Keeping a story minimal, or "spare," simply means removing detail. There are occasions in a corporate setting that demand a minimal story.

I was recently working with a multinational food products corporation in China. Along with my client, Samantha, I was working on a story that would convey the following key message: Consumers prefer small brands when it comes to making food choices.

Big brands like my client's are not a brand of choice. To convey this key message, Samantha and I decided to do some minimalist storytelling. The story was told by Samantha and, very simply, went like this:

Today, when it comes to making food choices, the country's ongoing food safety concerns are a big worry for consumers. Unfortunately, in such a situation a consumer prefers to buy from small brands like Green. [Please note: Green is not a real brand, of course; I have refrained from using a real brand for confidentiality reasons.]

You may wonder, who and what is Green?

In 2016, Karin Ho founded Green, one of China's first online farmers markets, to bring organic and local produce to families. Green is attempting to respond to consumers who are turning their backs on big food companies because they do not address issues such as transparency, obesity, inequality, and the climate crisis. Big brands are losing consumers. In China, when a consumer looks for safe food options, sadly big brands like ours are not their choice; Green is their choice.

Now, this is a minimal story with hardly any details. While we were getting ready with this story, Samantha had concerns I was already anticipating: "But is this even a story, Anjali? You've always told us that a story becomes effective when it has elements like setting, character, emotion, and so on." But having those details, on this occasion, for a corporate audience wasn't the right strategy. Why?

In the modern workplace, management has neither the time nor the patience to listen to maximal stories. If I want to hold the attention of my audience, I need to make my point in seconds, not minutes. But there's another, bigger problem. Even if my audience did take the time to listen to a fully developed narrative, my telling it in a detailed manner would get my listeners absorbed in the character, leaving them with no mental space to start thinking about the real issue—in this instance "Why isn't our big brand the brand of choice?" In other words, I don't want my audience to get too interested in character, setting, and so forth. A minimalist story was more effective in this case.

To be a strategic storyteller you will constantly have to decide when the story needs to be maximal and when minimal. The answer always lies with your audience. Who are you telling the story to? What is their connection point?

In a minimal story, connection comes from understanding that, if I really understand my audience—management in this case—I understand their connection points will come from the story proposing one of three outcomes. The story, and the change it proposes, will:

1. save the company **time**

2. enhance personal or organizational reputation (or **image**)

3. either **save money** or **make more money** for the organization.

Some tactics to make a story minimal are:

- Don't announce that you are about to tell a story. This can be achieved by simply avoiding the word *story* in the corporate boardroom.

- Make the story invisible. When you tell a story in a corporate boardroom, make it invisible by camouflaging it in between your key message/point at the beginning and your key message/point at the end. This can be done effectively by use of *segue lines*, which I cover later.

- Don't spend too much time developing or building your character. A character, the person in the story, in a minimal story is simply the carrier of the key message, not the most important feature. Mention the character, but don't dwell on the character. The focus is the key message/the point.

- Make sure the story is appropriate for senior stakeholders by leveraging the connection with TIM (remember: time, image, money!).

- Reduce the number of events. The sweet spot for a minimal story in terms of number of events is positioned right in the middle between a maximal story and an example. One of the less-known ways to make strategic stories stick in a corporate boardroom is to use a *story proposition*. We'll look at this in the next chapter, but first we have to take our pledge:

I pledge to remember and apply the following lessons:

- For management, we should make our stories minimal.
- The reason for minimal storytelling is not just time, but because management's connection points are different from those of other employees.
- Some of the tactics you can use to make your story minimal are:
    - Don't use the word *story*.
    - Don't develop your characters too much.
    - Make the story invisible.
    - Build the story proposition around TIM—time, image, money.
    - Reduce the number of events.

So back to story proposition!

CHAPTER 12

The Story Proposition

● ● ●

Estimated reading time: 12 minutes

What matters is not so much the story itself, but the story proposition.

The story proposition is an important aspect of the strategic story. Put simply, the story proposition is your explanation of why what is happening is happening in a story. The story could be about an overworked factory worker, but when you build your story proposition, you start looking for *why* is the worker overworked. Is he or she the only one who is overworked, or are there other workers in the same position? Is it the nature of work itself, or is it something about his or her way of working? When you are building your story proposition, you are trying to understand the complexity behind what is happening.

The key message or the point of the story is different from the proposition of the story.

The Difference Between the Key Message and the Story Proposition

Let me explain this difference using an example. First, we'll look at the key message, or point, made by a story.

My client wanted to make the point that technology is an equalizer. She was speaking to an audience that needed to hear this and understand that, in this technology-led world, their success is geography agnostic. Since she had just taken over the team, she wanted them to know a little bit about her and make the point as well. Her purpose was clear, and this is how she told the story strategically:

I grew up in Bangkok, Thailand, in a tech-oriented family. My dad is a professor in computer engineering. Growing up very close to internet technology, I tried very hard to differentiate myself from being associated with anything tech. I was the only family member who couldn't code and who had no interest in how computing technology could change our world.

My perspective shifted when I was 15. I went to study English during the summer months in the UK. It was 1993, when the internet had just made its way to Thailand. Since it was my first trip away from the country, my dad helped create my first email account and taught me how to use it. He told me that, when I reached the UK, I should try to find the nearest cybercafé and send emails to him. This was in 1993, before the advent of free internet and cell phones and laptops.

I was very excited about my first trip. I reached the UK and immediately the air smelled different. The hills and the trees also looked very different. The highlight was that I wasn't staying in a hotel or school dormitory but in the home of my English hosts, Barry and Cynthia. Barry and Cynthia were retirees, and they hosted foreign students who came to their city to study English. In our very first encounter, the conversation went like this. I asked them where in town I could use email, and they said, "E-what? What's that?" I explained to them that it was where you typed a letter on a computer and then pressed send. My email would then go through cyberspace and land on my dad's computer instantly. They said they had never heard anything like that before in their lives. Prior to this, they'd asked me a lot of questions about my country—including whether I had a TV, refrigerator, and electricity at home and whether I rode an elephant to school!

But in the very moment, it struck me: I was from a developing country with access to a developed country's technology—the internet. I was sitting in a developed country household with no access to the internet and where the occupants had very little understanding of a developing country. The moment empowered me to recognize the power of emerging technology and that access to internet technology could help equalize access to opportunities across the world.

This story tells us something about my client's character, but most importantly it makes a point. It doesn't end with statements glorifying my client's bravado of leaving her home and going overseas at the age of 15. You get that feeling that, too, but it's just a happy side effect, not the main point of the story.

Now the clear message of this story is that technology is an equalizer, but what makes it truly interesting is the story proposition that you can be from a developing country and have access to a developed country's technology, and vice versa. It is also not the most obvious point one would build on this story. The most obvious point here would have been to make this story about my client leaving home at the age of 15 and living with strangers and how brave she was to do that! I have no doubt she is brave, but through this story I can confidently say she is a strategic storyteller.

The key message is supported by the story proposition but is not the full explanation of how you arrived at that point—especially if the point is the non-obvious one. If my client just focused on her story, then what is the change we seek to make? Guaranteed, people feel connected to their leader because they have learned something about her. But by telling a story and making the point about technology being an equalizer, we are making the listeners adopt a point of view that, no matter where you are in the world, the same doors can be opened via technology.

When building a story proposition, there is one more thing to look out for. It is our tendency to make the most obvious point when using a story. We do this partly because we are either too lazy to interrogate further or because it confirms our biases. In *Blink: The Power of Thinking without Thinking*, Malcolm Gladwell talks about one of the pitfalls of storytelling being that we use can use the stories we tell ourselves to justify the choices we make. The corporate world has a similar issue where we find a story and in no time build a proposition to suit us around it. Your success, however, won't be driven by making the most obvious point, but by taking your audiences to places they won't go by themselves.

For example, recently I heard the former CEO of Cisco, John Chambers, sharing a story with Carmine Gallo, author of *Five Stars: The Communication Secrets to Get from Good to Great*, part of an interview posted on YouTube. Chambers was at a conference and didn't realize his wireless microphone was still on while talking to a woman after the session and so inadvertently revealed his dyslexia, which he had up to that point kept secret from his company and the world. Had he shared too much? He wondered.

When Chambers returned home that evening, he had several dozen voice messages and emails from employees who wanted to thank him for sharing his story. They told Chambers he had inspired and connected with them in a way he never had before. John Chambers had learned "the power of admitting my vulnerabilities and sharing my own story." As Chambers began to talk about dyslexia more openly, he realized what he had perceived as a weakness was actually the source of his greatest strength.

Now the most obvious propositions you can build around this story is: Our vulnerability is our strength, and we should all be vulnerable. However, when I shared Chambers' story with one of my clients and suggested that she build her own proposition around it, this is what she said:

[Chambers'] story resonates with me. As an Asian women leader, I have often struggled with the question: What is the right level of vulnerability I can share at work? I am cautious about displaying my shortfalls, setbacks, and emotional insecurities. I want to appear strong and capable as a leader.

The past few years have increased my awareness of how sharing vulnerability has become fashionable. There are more acknowledgments than ever of how showing vulnerability can be a way to build trust and psychological safety in the workplace, during a time when the outside world is less safe. More and more leaders have started to acknowledge their weaknesses. Some have done this more effectively than others.

What made this story special? I think it's that the CEO revealed his weakness unintentionally. This reinforces the idea that the purpose of revealing vulnerability shouldn't be self-serving. It wasn't shared as way of gaining popularity, or as an explanation for not delivering a certain outcome, but instead it was used solely to serve others.

As much as I find the concept of vulnerability comforting, the point of [Chambers'] story reminds me to not jump on the bandwagon of pouring out one's vulnerability without ensuring that you have some guardrails. These guardrails, in simple terms, are:

1. *What is the purpose of sharing?*
2. *How will this help the team in its journey toward becoming high performing?*

My client's theory is neither lazy, predictable, nor self-serving. She critically thinks through the situation and sets up an appropriate proposition around it.

This is exactly what every corporate professional should do when telling strategic stories.

A Simple Method for Telling Stories with a Unique Proposition

Step 1: Start with a clear key message you want to make.
Step 2: Tell a story that brings the key message to life.
Step 3: Now build your proposition around it.

If you have five minutes to tell a story, then use two and half minutes to tell the story and the rest to add in the proposition. Half and half!

We now know how to *find* a story and how to *tell* a story. However, we also need to be mindful of *who* is telling the story. We'll look at this in the next chapter after we take our pledge.

I pledge to remember and apply the following lessons:

- The story proposition is as important as the point or the key message of the story.
- The point is often a succinct, to-the-point line, while the proposition is the idea behind that point.
- The story proposition should not be built around the most obvious point you see in the story.
- If you are telling a strategic story, then your proposition should take up 50 percent of the telling time. It's as important as the story.

Now let's learn about who should tell the story.

CHAPTER 13

Who Should Tell the Story?

● ● ●

Estimated reading time: 4 minutes

Sometimes the storyteller matters more than the story.

In his book *Pre-Suasion: A Revolutionary Way to Influence and Persuade*, Robert Cialdini educates us on the fact that people are most influenced by those who are like them. In terms of storytelling, this is a lesson we have yet to learn. Somehow, our instincts inform us that only leaders can be relied on to tell a story. Perhaps this is due to the fact we see storytelling only as an inspirational tool and not as an influencing tool. But there are occasions when leaders are either less effective as storytellers or even completely the wrong person to tell a story. There are occasions when we have to find a teller who is like our audience—the commonality they have has the power to make a connection.

People Like Them Should Tell the Story

In 2015, I worked on a large digital transformation project with a technology brand. Working in collaboration with some team members, I got the change story ready and eventually it was time to prepare the brand's 70 or so leaders to tell the story to the ten thousand people who worked in the organization.

As we were working with the leaders, we made a decisive strategic decision—to create a force of story brand ambassadors who were all rank-and-file staff members. At that time, we had no idea this would become one of the reasons for the success of the change storytelling effort. There was investment made to teach the brand ambassadors how to tell a story. This investment paid off because the story reached every corner of the organization—the cafeteria, the smoking areas—the places where the corporate culture lives.

Normally in a corporate setting, it's the leader who's on the stage or at the front of the boardroom telling the story. If there are any concerns or objections or entrenched views, the audience won't say anything in front of the leader. However, in an informal environment, they do discuss these issues. In such cases, it really helps to invest time and money to create story brand ambassadors who have a complete understanding of the story to help cascade it through the organization.

Another occasion where this came to life for me was when I was working with an employment agency. We had built a bank of stories to tell migrant workers why they should get vaccinated against COVID-19. Of course, if a senior official were to advocate that migrant workers should get vaccinated, migrant workers would be skeptical. Therefore, I suggested the agency invest time and money in teaching selected migrant workers how to tell these stories. The influence potential, I pointed out, would be so much higher if the teller were someone just like the audience, and this turned out to be the case. Even the way in which stories are told can be democratized—through social channels or informal conversations in the workplace. The idea here is to take the story where it will be heard and be told by those who are somewhat like the people we are seeking to serve.

A change where you anticipate resistance is best achieved when you have stories told both from the top and from the bottom—from both the leadership and the people on the ground. The storytellers should never be just the leaders, but carefully chosen from the whole organization, depending on the occasion and desired outcome.

A couple of years ago, I rolled out a large artificial intelligence (AI) program in an organization. We prepared three groups of people to ensure that the story reached the more than 20,000 people who worked in the organization. The three groups were:

- the **CEO** who launched the AI narrative for the organization and the employees
- the **department heads** who made the AI narrative relevant for the departments and the employees

- the **AI ambassadors** who were employees from the ground level who understood the story very well and were able to overcome the kind of objections that only get voiced in casual environments—they were purely focused on making the narrative relevant for employees.

We have now learned the importance of choosing the right storyteller. It is now time for us to answer an important question: Do we only need to learn how to tell stories, or would we benefit from learning how to build *narratives*, too. Is there a difference? We'll learn this in the next chapter, after we have taken our pledge.

I pledge to remember and apply the following lessons:

- It is not just the leadership team who can and should tell stories.
- Story brand ambassadors help tell the story in informal environments where the corporate culture lives.
- For a change you anticipate will face resistance, it helps to have two-pronged approach, with both leaders and story brand ambassadors telling the story.

So let's now learn the difference between a story and a narrative.

CHAPTER 14

The Difference Between a Narrative and a Story

* * *

Estimated reading time: 6 minutes

A story can be just a moment in someone's life, but narratives are about someone's entire life including their hopes and aspirations for the future.

There are many great ways to define what a story is. Author Michael Lewis defines a story thus: "a story is—people and situations." I love the simplicity of this definition. It implies that character is central to a story. He or she must face a situation and then make choices that have consequences.

In a corporate setting, this definition is useful when we think of moments or anecdotes *from the past* that we can use to make a point, as in the story of my client in Chapter 11 in which she relates her going to the UK at the age of 15 in order to make her point that technology is an equalizer.

Real Stories are Lessons Rooted in the Past

A story in a corporate setting is articulating a moment from the past in a way that coveys a clear point and as result can make the change happen. Examples of the settings where we use a story to make a point are:

- values in action
- customer success

- where the point risks sounding like plain common sense, if not told like a story
- to establish cultural beliefs.

Here is an example of how one of my clients told a values in action story to her team. As you read through, note how the story is firmly rooted in the past.

What I want you to do is to go back to how you felt on the first day of your job. You probably felt a mixture of excitement and uncertainty. You had an orientation and got to know a lot of exciting things. One of the topics flashed on the orientation slides would have been "Company Values." You may not even remember this because most likely it meant nothing to you at that time.

Well, let me share with you my opinion on values back when I started my career. The website talked about values a lot, and there was even a whole page that formed a rather beautiful, framed piece of art perfect for decorating the office. That's it!

Nonetheless, it took 14 years of corporate experience for me to understand the value of values.

One of the things I used to be accused of in my career was seeking confirmation for every single decision I made. It was an inefficient process, but in my head and heart I wanted someone senior to agree with me. Quite frankly, I loved being right, and having a senior endorse my action plan was an affirmation that I was someone who always did the right thing. The trouble, though, was the time wasted in the process.

When I took on a leadership role, I thought it would be great if there was a manual I could give to my team to tell them all the right things to do and make us more efficient as a team. So, I decided to give them guidelines on what was acceptable and what was not. I called for a meeting with my team and said, "If you can support your decision as something made in an attempt to be creative and impactful, even if it is wrong, I will support you."

One of our company values was to be "creative and impactful." A very smart team member named Rachel said, "You mean stick to our company values?" I stopped and thought—yes, stick to our values! There it was, after 14 long years, I now finally understood how the company's values aligned with and contributed to its efficiency. I walked out of the boardroom thinking how I wished somebody had told me what exactly those values meant when I'd first started—how much more efficient I would have been!

Now, understanding the value of values is one thing, but how you communicate them is another. The best way to communicate what your values stand for is through stories. Here's an example: I recently had an opportunity to work with the communications team of a global agricultural manufacturing company on brand storytelling. One of the participants told this story of living values in action.

I was the account manager for a large account. I had a terrific relationship with my key client. We knew we would cover each other's back if needed. As a part of our working arrangement with them, we had to submit our invoices by a certain day of the month. If we were late, we incurred a big fine.

There was once I forgot to submit the invoice and my client said, "No problem, just backdate it. That way you'll avoid incurring unnecessary fines." My initial response was "Oh, thanks so much," but after I'd said that I kept thinking of our company value "Do the right thing" and I knew that what I was about to do certainly wasn't acting in line with the company values. I called the client back and said, "Thank you so much for offering to backdate the invoice but I want to act in line with our values. We'll proceed to pay the fine."

I did get into trouble at work for forgetting and incurring unnecessary costs, but in a matter of months the client called and increased our scope, saying, "We like working with people like you who are trustworthy and will always do the right thing."

Stories Are Great but Not Enough

There are so many stories like these we can use in a corporate setting to make a point, but it's not enough of a communication tool to give everyone a common vision. What can we use to show them what the *future* would look like, unlike a story which is usually a lesson from the *past*?

About five years ago, Stanford Graduate Business School posted a YouTube video of Indra Nooyi, Former PepsiCo Chairman and CEO, and Doug McMillon, Walmart President and CEO, having a conversation. At one point in the conversation, Nooyi is asked by McMillon about change in an organization, and she responds by sharing a story about the time when she was trying to change the product portfolio of

PepsiCo from a "fun for you" product line to "better for you" product line; she wanted the values of the product portfolio to be more closely tied with agriculture and health. At that time, PepsiCo's employees were likely wondering why change was needed at all, as PepsiCo was already doing so well selling the current products they had. Nooyi asserts, in response, that the leader's biggest challenge is to make a change before it is too late to make it.

This response clearly tells you why, sometimes, you need a narrative, not a story. You need a narrative to show the future others don't see yet. Narratives are forward-looking. They help people see themselves becoming successful as the organization becomes successful. Narratives bring everyone onto the same page and propel the change.

There are times, however, when you will feel confused: Should I build a narrative or tell a story? But that's for the next chapter. For now, let's take this chapter's pledge.

I pledge to remember and apply the following lessons:

- Stories are lessons from the past; narratives are forward-looking.
- Stories almost always have a character; narratives may or may not have a character.
- A story can be part of a narrative.
- Generally speaking, narrative unfolds over a longer timeframe.
- Stories make a point; narratives ask people to adopt new ways of doing things.

CHAPTER 15

A Strategic Choice

NARRATIVE OR STORY?

• • •

Estimated reading time: 4 minutes

While stories can make a point, they don't point toward the future.

While you now understand the difference between a narrative and a story, your success with corporate storytelling is dependent on your strategic choice between the two. Before we explore this, I want to first share with you a potential pitfall that can arise.

A Potential Pitfall When Choosing Between a Narrative and a Story

Let's say that you work for a semiconductor chip manufacturing company. You are leading a team of close to 50 senior engineers who are all overworked. You understand the difficulty of the situation, and as a leader you are worried about the fact the engineers will not be able to sustain these working conditions long term. As a result, you have hired 50 new engineers straight out of college who have the knowledge but not necessarily the experience in your industry. Your thought process is that over time they will gain experience and things will become better. Except they don't.

You're now in a meeting with the senior engineers, and one of them says, "It takes more time to do the job if I take a young engineer with me. On top of doing the job, I have to spend time explaining the job to them. It is not help but more work."

After you listen to the engineer, it would be easy to fall into the trap of giving your point of view on why they should include the young engineer and insisting upon the long-term benefits (we'll look at exactly why it's a trap below). But instead, here is what a client of mine did. He told a story as a response:

Last November, I was sitting in a meeting room with a group of senior engineers and managers working on one of the biggest issues in our network. Everyone was struggling to identify the root cause, including our global team members. We're trained to always "go to the point of operation"—the factory. So, the manager, along with the equipment engineers, decided to go to the factory, open up the machine, and start methodically collecting data for analysis. Eventually, after a few days of intensive data collection, we were able to find the source of the contamination. Problem solved.

But it wasn't just the problem of the contamination that was solved that day; there was something even bigger and better that happened. One of the engineers who went to the factory was a young engineer who had joined our organization two months before the event took place. The other one was a very senior engineer. Because of the vision and the courage of the senior engineer, he was able to include the young engineer from the beginning, contributing to the troubleshooting work, and thus reducing the workload on the senior engineer. On top, this also accelerated the young engineer's learning. And now, eight months after she joined our organization, she's leading a few portfolios. Now, some of you will say that maybe this is a special case; not every young engineer is able to do this. I was having a discussion with another director two months ago who leads one of the highest-performing teams. I was expecting him to tell me how experienced his team is. To my surprise, 70 percent of the engineers in his team have been employees for less than two years. They have built a culture of performance based on the culture of inclusion.

Clearly, my client is telling a story here, not a narrative—rooted in lessons drawn from the past, not looking into the future. But the question is how did he make this strategic choice? The guidelines below may help.

How You Make the Choice to Tell a Story and Not a Narrative

- In the example above, my client told his story in response to *a question asked*. Often, stories are a good choice for responding to specific questions.
- It takes *less time* to tell a story than to share a narrative. Therefore, in time-poor situations, and where a story will suffice, make this choice.
- The *nature of the setting* you are in will also inform the choice. Informal and conversational environments are conducive to stories. Narratives are usually shared in more formal environments.
- Consider whether your response needs to cover where we have come from, where we are, and where we are going. If the answer is no, then a story will do just fine.

Environments where I would choose a narrative over a story include:

- launching a change in an organization
- a new product rollout
- a new strategy rollout.
- a new campaign rollout.
- when asking for funds or resources for a new initiative
- simply answering why we are doing what we are doing.

A story is a good solution for helping us understand something better, while a narrative is a good solution for taking us toward a future we want to be a part of.

Building narratives is the subject of Part III of this book, but first let's take our final pledge for this part.

I pledge to remember and apply the following lessons:

- Stories are a good solution for helping us understand something better.
- Narratives are a good solution for taking us toward a future we want to be a part of.
- Stories make a point, but narratives show me the path ahead.
- Situations where we should tell a story include:
  - responding to specific questions
  - when we are in a time-poor situation and when a story will suffice
  - in informal and conversational environments.
- Situations where we should share a narrative include:
  - launching a change in an organization
  - a new product rollout.
  - a new strategy rollout.
  - a new campaign rollout
  - when asking for funds or resources for a new initiative
  - simply answering why we are doing what we are doing.

CHAPTER 16

Examples of Storytelling

• • •

Estimated reading time: 9 minutes

Let's put stories to work.

Before we proceed to the next and final part of the book, I want to share some examples that illustrate the ideas I have covered so far.

Story 1: Making Your Points Personal with Stories

A client of mine needed to make the point that digital is changing the way we work and live. Both of us were aware that the fastest way to be ignored when talking about digital transformation is to start out by stating what the audience already knows—for instance, by simply saying just those words: "Digital is changing the way we work and live." Sadly, many digital transformation presentations start with a similar sentence. While it is undoubtedly correct statement, it is also one that can be ignored. In my client's case, we realized that we needed to make it personal and tell a story making a point about exactly *how* digital is changing the way we work and live. And this is the story we told:

I want to start off today by taking you through my morning before I arrived in the office.

I woke up around 6 a.m. this morning, just in time to have a chat with my son who lives in the USA. So, my 6 a.m. is 6 p.m. for him. I used Skype to call him. I then bought a book I have been meaning to read from Amazon and used PayPal for the payment. I then asked Amazon Alexa to read me the news headlines. I then got ready, ordered a Grab [a private car service in

Southeast Asia] and got to the office. On my way up to the office, I bought a coffee from a café downstairs and paid using PayWave.

In just under two hours, I had used Skype, Amazon shopping, Amazon Alexa, Grab, PayPal, and PayWave.

The story created a personal connection and made a point, we engaged the audience, and most importantly, via the story, the audience *felt* digital transformation versus just knowing about it.

REFLECTIONS

Is there a personal story you could tell that makes the point how digital is changing the way we work and work?

Can you think of any message that is correct but runs the risk of being ignored if not wrapped up in a story? For example:

- Sustainability is the key to our success.

- The climate crisis is here.

- The mental health and wellbeing of our staff are key to our productivity.

What are some of your personal experiences that can bring these messages to life?

Story 2: Making Your Audience Experience the Problem

A group of government officials I worked with had come up with an idea to launch a website to inform travelers about what they can and can't bring into the country. They were required to present this idea to a group of senior officials in order to receive sponsorship for the project.

Their proposed presentation began with explaining the problem, and the officials projected the problem statement onto a slide:

For people traveling into the country, there is no single source to find out what they are allowed or not allowed to bring.

After establishing the problem statement, they started showing the prototype of the website they had developed.

There was a problem with this approach. Those listening, like myself, immediately wondered why we wouldn't just Google this information. Was it was really so complicated that we needed a whole website to address the issue? Such thoughts risked mushrooming and becoming a distraction, so this is how we changed the presentation.

The presentation now began with a photograph, taken at customs, projected onto the screen, which remained there as my client told the following story:

A gentleman named Richard is crossing customs and is asked by the customs officer to open his bag. Customs officers find 7 kilos of a fortified health food in Richard's bag. Richard is informed by the customs officer he is not allowed to bring this amount into the country, something that he is shocked to hear.

At this point, the presenter asked the audience to use their mobiles to find out whether this information was available online. Of course, no one could find it quickly. This was how we *demonstrated* the problem versus simply *stating* the problem—using storytelling.

REFLECTION

Think of situations where, instead of just articulating the problem you are trying to solve, you can make people *feel* the problem by giving them an experience.

For example, recently a client of mine who had some grants to allocate for new startups found that no one was applying for the grant. We soon found out that the reason for this was that the application process was simply too arduous, and to tell the story of this we got the management to experience the application process for themselves. This then led to a change of portal for filing the application.

Story 3: Taking People into Familiar Experiences

There was a senior management meeting coming up, and a strong presenter had been chosen to lead the presentation. A day before the presentation, I was sitting with the entire team responsible for managing the upcoming presentation to the management. The purpose of the presentation was to make a case why the organization needed to curate a change story for a major change it was going through. The team was prepared, they had relevant content, but their delivery still needed work. Here was the advice I gave:

The presenter is being brave enough to not use PowerPoint as a crutch, but at one stage of the presentation he says, "There are a lot more semiconductor chips in a car than there used to be, and it is one of the reasons why demand for chips has increased."

This is a just set of words that could easily be ignored. What if he were to say something like this?

"Not that long ago, when we needed to reverse-park our cars, we had to be skilled enough to do it without bumping into anything. But now we have reverse-park sensors to help us park our cars safely. As soon as we are close to something, we hear a beep … Our semiconductor chips are the reason these reverse-park sensors work. Over the years, cars have gained a lot of new features, all supported by our semiconductor chips."

At this stage, if you can show this visual on the screen, it will help reinforce your point (Figure 16.1). The visual demonstrates the amount of features cars have now.

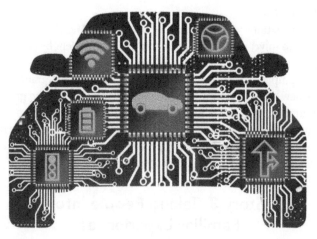

Figure 16.1 Features of a car supported by a semiconductor chip
(Source: Alamy)

Most people have experienced reverse car parking and the enhanced features of a car. When you take your audiences into a familiar experience via storytelling, it sticks, resonates, and makes sense, not just to you but to your audiences, too.

REFLECTION

Think which of your presentation statements are important but can be ignored. After you have listed those, think about some of the familiar experiences you can take the audience to where they can understand the point you are making. Your theoretical concept becomes a practical concept.

Story 4: Building Confidence with Storytelling

Roxanne, the leader of the change management function of an organization I was consulting for, recognized that, when SAP (systems, applications, and products) implementation takes place, people will resist. Therefore, she decided to tell the story of how SAP would lead to a better future even before the team was introduced to the software. This was an excellent approach because it would gradually familiarize the group with this unknown beast called SAP.

The first tactic was to simply look where else SAP had been implemented and whether the result had been good. A story from another person in another organization was used. This is the story told by another client which we shared with Roxanne's team:

When I took up the role of leading SAP services in my company I found several areas for potential value optimization. There were software licenses that weren't being used yet incurring maintenance costs, there were data centre systems that were unused but not decommissioned, as well a multiple implementations of similar systems. From where I stood it seems that we could deliver significant costs savings for the company.

The management had asked me to take stock of our SAP landscape and wherever possible, terminate unused software, decommission unused systems and consolidate near-duplicate installations, in order to find multimillion-dollar cost savings.

I wanted to ensure we built a foundation for a sustainable value optimization program and so adopted a structured methodology. We chose to adopt a "Business Transformation Management Methodology" after consulting SAP. This would support improvement of IT operations and required engagement with stakeholders from SAP support and some other teams. The approach to this engagement was based on "design thinking," which integrates the needs of stakeholders, the possibilities of technology, and the requirements for business success. This seemed an appropriate approach because it considered both usability from a human experience perspective and viability from a business perspective.

At the end of the process we were able to identify 82 improvement opportunities, which would potentially deliver tangible as well as intangible value for the company. We also ended almost 40 software licenses and decommissioned 25 unused systems, whilst consolidating two systems with multiple installations. Progress continues and further opportunities are being identified.

While this story built confidence in SAP, people would still not see its relevance to their own life. The next step was to take real stories relating the difficulties people were facing and share with them how SAP would provide the solution. You may not know exactly how it will solve the problem, but you have a fair idea of the kind of problems it will solve.

There are a few things to note here:

Since this communication is about reshaping the future, asking people to stop doing what they are doing and adopt new ways of doing things to change the future, this example is more suited to being called a narrative versus a story.

Furthermore, notice how a story from another organization will not be enough in this case. We can build credibility by sharing others' examples, but connection only gets built when I see my own problem. And it is the combination of connection (from my own problem) and credibility (from others' examples) that leads to the building of confidence.

REFLECTION

What new ways of working are you trying to get the people in your organization to adopt? Which other company's story can you tell to build credibility?

What is the story from your own organization you can tell to build connection?

This brings us to the end of Part II of this book. It's now time for us to adopt a new strategic storytelling identity: that of the visionary who builds and tells narratives.

PART III

How to Tell a Strategic Corporate Narrative

Becoming a visionary storyteller

This part of Strategic Storytelling *is about setting a vision for the future, and when I think of this storytelling identity, I think above all of the Black civil rights leader Martin Luther King Jr., who led people to envision their future success and inspired them to take the actions necessary to achieve that future. King was a visionary storyteller indeed.*

Figure 17.1 A visionary who tells narratives to make a change happen

CHAPTER 17

Why Narratives Now?

* * *

Estimated reading time: 8 minutes

> *Things have always changed but not at the unprecedented speed they change now, and that's why narratives matter now more than ever.*

Let's revisit what we've covered so far.

In Part I, we learned how adopting the identity of a marketer teaches us the importance of connection, which is fundamental to strategic storytelling.

In Part II, we learned strategic storytelling is not reserved for leaders in organizations, a common myth that still needs debunking. You can be a strategic storyteller from your orientation day on. First, you adopt the identity of a reflective and journalist storyteller who is focused on finding stories. Then you adopt the identity of a reporter to tell those stories effectively. Take these actions and you are a strategic storyteller from the day you start work.

In Part III, we are going to learn about the fifth identity—the visionary storyteller. Someone who helps people see the future and, more importantly, see their own success in that imagined future. The tool the visionary uses to make a change happen by showing a successful future is the strategic corporate narrative.

Let's get started.

Agreement Is Not Alignment

Most modern-day leaders rely on making the change happen solely by using clear, concise, and credible communication. In doing so, they may get the agreement from people on the desired change but will not get align-ment. There is a difference: Agreement means you nod your head and say, "I agree"; alignment makes you act in the direction of the desired change.

Agreement + Alignment = Action = Desired change takes place

Agreement – Action (a head nod is hardly an action!) = Nothing changes

Sadly, agreement is the common conclusion of corporate meetings because it is a convenient outcome which lowers the probability of any conflict. And, in some cases, the agreement is genuine but not enough of a force to take an action. We all agree that polishing off a tub of ice cream in one sitting is bad, but on occasion we still give in to that craving. In this case, there was likely no alignment.

Strategic Corporate Narratives: The Vessel to a Successful Future

For agreement to shift into alignment we need to show people the new identities they will take on because they have helped change happen. The vessel carrying our audience to a successful future is the strategic corporate narrative.

Strategic corporate narratives help leaders reshape their employees' worldviews. It makes them feel and understand that the change will benefit them as well and is not just a proposition they have to adopt simply for the sake of the business's profitability.

To help you understand the point I'm making here, I will turn to one of my own experiences:

I was helping a client develop a change narrative. I was still in the discovery phase of the project and was invited by the client to attend sessions where the change was being communicated. One day I was sitting in a large auditorium of a large multinational where the CEO was delivering a message to rank-and-file employees highlighting there would be a change in the organization. They would be getting rid of the 30-year-old legacy Customer Relationship Management (CRM) system and replacing it with a new-age system.

The CEO then gave the reasons for the change:

- *growing competition*
- *ever more complex ways of working*

- *tendency of employees to work in silos*
- *loss of market share.*

After the meeting was over, I asked one of the employees, "Do you remember and, more importantly, understand what the CEO said in his speech?" Her candid response was: "The only thing I remember is something about the loss of market share, but I don't get paid enough to worry about that. I agree we need to change, but it doesn't mean I have the desire, energy, or the will to do so."

Was I shocked by the response? No, I would have thought the same way if I was her. I would nod in agreement but would not align with the change. Remember, the choice to change is always the prerogative of our audience.

This anecdote throws a spotlight on a very common issue in an organizational setting where an immense effort is made by the CEO and internal communication team to come up with a clear, concise, and credible message to drive a change. They give reasons for the change but never achieve the desired change.

As Donald Calne, a Canadian neurologist has taught us, in his book *Within Reason*: "The essential difference between emotion and reason is that emotion leads to action while reason leads to conclusions." The conclusion in the above case is the nod the employee gave when she agreed that change was required. The CEO's clear, concise, and credible communication, however, lacked the emotion to make a connection and move agreement into action. The emotional connection could have been made if the CEO's communication had painted the picture of a future where the employee was successful in a successful organization.

Emotional connection is the force that propels strategic corporate narratives.

Strategic Corporate Narratives and the Speed of Change

We have always needed strategic corporate narratives, but today we need them more than ever. Yesterday they were important, but today they are necessary—and mostly because of the unprecedented speed of change we are experiencing. For example:

- Factories are becoming smart factories.
- The focus of food products is shifting from taste to health.
- Radiologists are being replaced by robots.
- Pandemics like COVID-19 have changed the way we work.

Things are shifting fast, including the very nature of how we experience change. In his book *Thank You for Being Late*, US commentator Thomas Friedman highlights how change has always been with us, but that now the speed of change is daunting.

Broadly speed of change matters to the modern-day leader in a couple of ways:

- Information has been democratized because it is available to everyone via the internet. In the past, we typically respected leaders because of their experience, which gave them the knowledge and information others didn't have. But now, knowledge is just an effective Google search away. So, what is the role of a leader? The answer is: To be a visionary and share the strategic corporate narratives that drive change. A leader's ability to influence is far more valuable than the knowledge they have.
- We have always expected change, but what we didn't expect was that rampant change would be the only constant. This breakneck speed of change has put today's leaders in a difficult position because every organizational change is accompanied by resistance from the people you need the most to make the change happen—your employees. So, what is the role of a leader in this ever-changing environment? Once again, it is to be a visionary and share strategic corporate narratives, and once again, their ability to influence is far more valuable than the knowledge they have.

Strategic Corporate Narratives: A Way to Succeed in a Fast-Changing World

Now, imagine having to motivate people to change in a fast-changing environment where you are not even the keeper of all the information, based on the same old tricks.

Strategic corporate narratives can't change the speed of change. Granted.

They can't ensure knowledge is based on experience alone. Granted.

Yet they do give the modern leader the highest chance of success in this ever-changing world where we need more than knowledge to be respected, heard, and make a change happen.

As Indra Nooyi, ex-CEO of PepsiCo, expressed in a conversation with Doug McMillon, Walmart president and CEO, the most challenging job of the leader is to look ahead to the future and change things before its too late.

A strategic corporate narrative helps make this happen. It's a communication that, when heard, makes the person *want* to move toward the change, instead of *having* to.

Success with Strategic Corporate Narratives Requires Skill and Spotting Opportunities

It takes more than just knowing how to build strategic corporate narratives to achieve the desired outcome, however. For a long time, I thought that, if I taught my clients how to tell a strategic corporate narrative, they would learn it and tell it. Only a lack of skill was stopping them. But there was another roadblock: The conventional ways of communicating are so engrained in corporate settings that we don't even see the alternative ways available to us. We are victims to our defaults, to well-worn mental pathways, to old and predictable ways of communicating. Even though my clients now knew how to tell a strategic corporate narrative, they failed to spot opportunities to tell them.

The opportunity to share a narrative doesn't come with a drumroll. It's always there. But you have to spot it.

So, before we learn how to develop strategic corporate narratives, it's important to explore how we miss making a change happen by failing to see the opportunities to do so. But before we do, let's take our pledge for this chapter.

125

I pledge to remember and apply the following lessons:

- A leader's goal is not to get agreement but to get alignment.
- Agreement without action is useless.
- For too long we have relied on clear, concise, and credible reasons and messages to make change happen. This, however, is not a sound strategy.
- Today, the role of a leader is to be a visionary because knowledge is democratized and the speed of change is the only certainty.

Now, let's move on to why we miss spotting opportunities to tell a strategic corporate narrative.

CHAPTER 18

Missed Opportunities for Telling Strategic Corporate Narratives

• • •

Estimated reading time: 8 minutes

Even if we tell the right narrative, we often do so using the wrong frame.

In a corporate organization, a desired change might be an IT conversion, a department merger, an acquisition, or anything else that requires our teams to stop doing the things they are comfortable with and start doing the things not familiar to them. The default way to announce a change is to give people the reasons, benefits, advantages, and knowledge for why the change is needed and what they have to do to facilitate the change. This makes the rank-and-file staff feel like all change initiatives are driven by profitability, and that management has no care or concern for the people on the ground who are impacted by the change. This, of course, leads to subpar work and implementation.

Even if we know this by default, we continue to frame the change in a dusty way that is bound to be ineffective. This is because we have failed to see the opportunity tell a narrative.

Examples of Missed Opportunities to Share a Narrative

Here are two change messages I have come across that were delivered by the leadership teams of organizations. Take note of the framing.

"We have to change our system because we are losing market share."

"We have to change our factory into a smart factory because we have to increase our productivity."

If I were a rank-and-file employee and heard these as reasons for change, I'd tell myself a story: "This change is hard for me. It impacts me because I must learn a new system and learn to work with machines. There's no upside for me."

In each case, the leadership's framing of change messages (mostly in reasons of profitability) makes no connection with the audience, and therefore hinders change. There were clearly missed opportunities here. We need to extend our horizons and ask ourselves: What success does this change bring to our employees and the causes they care about, such as the planet and society.

When we dig deeper, we realize that business profitability doesn't have to go hand in hand with lack of care for employees. The reason we don't talk about employee benefits alongside business profitability is because we haven't used our imaginations to find the right story. The right story is the story our audience wants to listen to. As narrators, all we need to do is find that story and tell it. Entrepreneur, bestselling author, and speaker Seth Godin advocates that great stories don't teach us anything new—they agree with our existing worldviews. If an employee comes to work to be successful, then if you tell a story that shows the employee being successful, you have a great story. If an employee comes to work wanting to help the planet and society, then if you tell a story that shows the employee being successful doing just that, you have a great story.

The purpose of the narrative is to align with what our employees are already thinking.

So, instead of saying,

"We have to change our system because we are losing market share."

we might say,

We are changing our system because the current system was built 20 years ago and it can no longer serve the needs of today's customers. We are constantly finding our rank-and-file staff in difficult customer conversations because the current system is slow and takes several minutes to provide our staff with the information they need. I have witnessed many of our staff going through such embarrassing situations, and the new system will change this for the staff. They want and need to serve the customers better. That's how they feel successful.

Instead of explaining,

We have to change our factory into a smart factory because we have to increase our productivity.

we might say,

We are changing our factory into a smart factory because the rise in technology has rapidly increased the demand for our product. What we must produce today is four times more than what we had to produce two years ago. But, in these two years, our staff strength has remained the same. So, the only way we have achieved this growth in manufacturing is by making our staff work a lot more than they should. I have witnessed many of our staff working overtime and over the weekends. How about we automate this heavy work and help our team become valuable human analysts and strategists?

Can you feel the difference?

Communication, if not relevant, falls on deaf ears, but, if relevant, becomes the force of connection.

We have long relied on reasons and knowledge to drive change in an organization. Sadly, this reliance on reasons and knowledge betrays us and does not lead to the desired outcome. To ask people to stop doing the things they are comfortable with and start trying to do things in a new way not familiar to them does not connect. And, as we know, if there is no connection, there is no action.

We will keep missing opportunities to make a desired change happen if we fail to replace pretty PowerPoint presentations with strategic corporate narratives. Organizational change specialist John Kotter says most people think change happens when we first analyze a problem, then we think about how we can solve it and finally we make the change. However, in Kotter's experience he says the actual process is that we see a situation which produces a reaction or feeling in us, and that gives us the fire to make a change. Now, what is interesting is the insight of the "the fire to CHANGE." *Knowledge* about the change fails to ignite the fire, but *feelings* about the change do ignite the fire.

Be a Change Nurse, Not a Change Doctor

I often use a healthcare analogy to help people understand this concept better. In the healthcare environment, doctors treat illness and injury, while nurses care for individuals, families, and communities. Doctors treat, and nurses care.

In driving an organizational change, what nurses do matters more than what doctors do. We need people to be motivated to make the change.

Don't be a change doctor who diagnoses the problem and treats it. Be the change nurse who not only gives patients their drugs on time but also finds meaning in their feelings and cares about their recovery. People accept changes they're emotionally invested in.

Parallels Between Parenting and Managing a Change

Just look at something as simple as becoming a parent. Having a child is perhaps one of the biggest changes one can experience. Yet, we love our children, look after them, want the best for them. We are always motivated to change ourselves for our child's benefit.

The same isn't true for an organizational change. We are given reasons, support, training, and more to help us change but we are still unmotivated.

Why this disparity?

We are emotionally invested in our children, but we are not emotionally invested in organizational change.

When it comes to our children, there is no strategy, no plan, and no data analytics. Only their happiness matters. We have unconditional love for our children because of our survival instinct to take our species forward. To this goal, we tend to ignore anything that doesn't help us survive or thrive. We ignore much of the information written on an airline safety card but will carefully listen to an attendant talking about flight time, exit points, and information on whether we are expecting turbulence. It's all about the emotional connection.

Organizations can create emotional investment, too. But that doesn't mean tricks. Emotion in communication doesn't have to be achieved by manipulation, but through the force of a strategic corporate narrative.

You are now well and truly ready to learn about the structure of a strategic corporate narrative. But before that let's take a pledge.

I pledge to remember and apply the following lessons:

- A change proposition is often meaningless to employees because it focuses entirely on business profitability.
- An opportunity to share a strategic corporate narrative is often missed because we fail to see an opportunity due to our entrenched ways of communicating in a corporate setting.
- A successful change is not a result of careful analysis of the problem, then finding a solution and then asking people to change. It is a result of making people see something, feel something, and then giving them the fire in their belly to want to change.
- People accept changes they're emotionally invested in.

Now, let's move on to the all-important *structure* of a strategic corporate narrative.

CHAPTER 19

Assembling a Maximal Narrative

PART 1

● ● ●

Estimated reading time: 16 minutes

Just as with stories, the apparent spontaneity of a narrative is a fallacy.

There are two types of narrative structures available to us: maximal and minimal narratives.

As the names suggest, the level of detail required in the minimal narrative is less than in the maximal narrative. The kind of narrative you choose depends on who you are telling it to and the time you have to tell it in. I will talk more about choosing the appropriate narrative structure in the later part of this chapter. For the moment, let's define each more precisely:

A **maximal narrative** motivates change, no doubt, but it goes into the detail of what is causing the need for us to change. It provides detail, data, and insights. It shows a bright future where the audience is successful. Skeptical and analysis-driven minds love these kinds of narratives. They take time and are perfectly suited to employees or for internal presentation purposes—the audience you work with every day.

The **minimal narrative** is conceptual in nature. Think of it as being like a mood board for a video. Before you make a video, you often present a mood board in which you share the look and the feel of the video and the inspiration behind it. It talks about exactly what the video is trying to do and the purpose of the video, but it doesn't get into the exact details of how the problem will be solved: for example, a commercial for a washing powder that can turn your soiled shirt into a clean shirt in no time because you are time poor and need the shirt every day.

Figure 19.1 The maximal narrative

You often see these types of narratives in senior boardroom presentations and quick corridor chats because they tend to be great for time-poor environments. They lack details but give you a good idea of the problem you are trying to solve. They are successful, not because we have given a detailed solution to the problem, but because we have created immense resonance by telling the story of the problem people are facing and introducing the solution. They are often told to people who work *on* the business, not *in* the business, or to customers who simply want their problems solved.

If minimal narratives are the mood board, then maximal narratives are the frame-by-frame storyboard.

It is time to dig deeper into both narrative structures, guiding you through the ten steps of the maximal narrative. I have divided the ten steps into three different chapters—because I want to keep the promise I made earlier to keep the chapters short, so that you can read and feel you are making progress despite your busy schedules.

Also, the steps are a guide, not a rigid rulebook. If you don't need all ten steps, don't use them! For a visual guide to the ten steps, please refer to Figure 19.1.

Step 1: Provide Your Listeners with a New Identity That They Desire

In 2001, in Singapore, I walked into an amphitheater with ten other young women. All of us were newly recruited flight attendants for Singapore Airlines. It was our first day of work, and we were about to start our orientation. I was expecting someone to show up on the stage and share the company vision, mission, values, and so on. I had attended company orientations before and thought I knew what they were like.

But there was something different happening here. No one showed up, and instead a screen rolled down at the back of the stage. After a few awkward seconds, a video played. I didn't blink once as I watched the video; I had goosebumps, and my eyes were teary. The one-minute video was called: "Across the World with the Singapore Girl" (you can still watch this video on YouTube today).

In just a minute, the video did a brilliant job of showing me the identity I would form as a result of being a Singapore Airlines flight attendant. What followed after that day was a challenging training schedule, high standards of grooming, early reporting times, detailed safety procedures, the struggle of understanding foreign accents and, of course, homesickness (I was born and raised in India). But I learned to deal with all of that because I knew that, if I got through it, I would be the girl I saw in the video.

The story of the "Singapore Girl" was a nudge toward my new identity. Because of that story, I was able to work hard and change. The story fueled my intrinsic motivation to adopt my new identity. Similarly, when implementing a change within a corporate setting, it's important to show people the new identity they will form as a result of the change, and then the hard work required to change will follow. The story is what sets the vision for the change and fuels people with the motivation to keep going when things get tough. It brings fanatical discipline to stick to the path.

It's not uncommon for me to hear from my clients they have spent millions setting up a new digital transformation infrastructure but then struggle with its adoption across the organization. Mostly, the lack of adoption is due to lack of a concomitant new identity for the stakeholders. Instead of making an effort to form the identity, they get caught up in outcomes and processes.

In his book *Atomic Habits*, author James Clear mentions how, when we are trying to change our habits, we focus on outcomes and process as a default. For example, running a marathon is an outcome and training is the process involved in achieving the outcome. But the true intrinsic motivation to change comes from forming a new identity. The prouder you are of your new identity, the more you will be driven to make the change happen. Running a marathon is an outcome, not an identity. "I am a marathoner" is an identity. Writing a book is a goal, not an identity. "I am an author" is the identity.

Just like the video I watched in 2001, stories are a great way to transport people toward their desired futures. A modern digital leader who wants to shift their traditional manual labor-based organization into a digital-first one has to know how to tell this story. If a leader fails to do so, it is highly unlikely they'll rise to a new level.

The story you tell is the nudge to individual enrollment in the change. It helps your employees willingly say things like this:

- "I want to be part of the workforce of the future."
- "I want to be a cybersecurity professional or a data scientist."

When you get enrollment from many people within your organization, alignment happens. One by one, you'll see everyone aligning to chase their new identity. When alignment happens, the desired change takes place.

In summary, before you embark on your next organizational change, ask the following questions:

- What is the new identity people will form because of this change?
- What is the story I can tell to transport them to the future holding their new identity?
- Will the story I tell get me enrollment and alignment?

In their book *Made to Stick*, Chip and Dan Heath share the story of Crystal Jones, an American primary school teacher who wanted to spark a desire for change in her students. On taking over her class of first graders, Crystal set them a target: "By the end of the year, you are going to be third graders!" She duly informed her students that they were not ordinary pupils but "scholars." She taught them what it means to be a scholar and encouraged them to use this term when talking to one another. When someone happened to visit the class and asked why the pupils addressed each other in this way, the whole class responded in chorus that "A scholar is someone who lives to learn and who is good at it!"

When spring came, tests showed that the class had already reached the level required for second grade, so Jones threw a graduation party. From this point on, the students were to think of themselves as "second-graders" and the kids enjoyed immensely referring to themselves as such for the rest of the year. By June, Jones had reached her objective: In terms of scholastic achievement, 90 percent of her class were at third-grade level or higher!

If Jones had told her pupils that, by the end of the year, they would have covered fractions and decimals, it would have meant nothing to them. Instead, she chose a goal that would resonate with small children: 'I'm going to be a third-grader!" She nudged her students to have a new identity. It was a goal with emotional resonance.

Here are some examples of how I have worked with organizations to transform their purpose of change to new identities:

Purpose	Identity
Reduce the loss in market share	To become a *trusted advisor*
Continue our operations in Singapore	To become the *workforce of the future*
Reduce the time spent in non-value-added work	To be a *respected supply chain professional*

As you can see, each identity considers what is best for employees. It is people-centric, not productivity- or profitability-centric. To define a new identity, you need immense clarity on the identity that will be desirable to people. This also digs deep, so saying, for example, "This change will help you save you time" is not enough. You have to say what saving time will lead to for your employees.

For example, automation will save time. This saved time can be used to analyze data and influence strategic decisions. When you can influence decisions for better business outcomes, you become a trusted advisor.

Let's look at the layers here:

Top layer	Automation saves time.
Second layer	Time gives you an ability to analyze data.
Third layer	When you analyze data, you can influence decisions.
Fourth layer	When you influence decisions for better business outcomes, you become a trusted advisor.

Maximal narratives start with a clearly articulated *new identity*.

Imagine a CEO standing in front of five hundred employees delivering a maximal narrative and starting with the identity:

Today, I am here to talk about making you the workforce of the future.

After making this promise, the narration that follows is all about the audience. The second line the leader will say is:

In the next X minutes, I will take you through the path for you to become a workforce of the future.

You have now started with a strong nudge to new identity.

The next step is to build an affinity with the narrator him- or herself.

Step 2: Engage Your Audience with a Leader's Personal Story

In 2018, one of my clients, the managing director and president of a large semiconductor manufacturer, was rolling out a new strategy. Employee morale was down because they had been informed that China (which contributed 50 percent of the company's regional revenue) would not be part of their region. They needed to find ways to achieve the same results without the biggest revenue contributor.

My client is a strategic business leader. He had looked at what his region had versus what it didn't have now—in other words, what the company's identity would be if it excluded China versus what it would be if it included China. He also needed to determine how best to leverage the uniqueness of the region and drive great outcomes. Their new strategy was based on a simple principle:

If we leverage our own unique strengths, we can have a very bright future even without China.

Now, if my client had delivered this message as it was, it would have sounded almost cliché and would therefore have run the risk of falling on deaf ears. To avoid the trap, my client leveraged the strength of his personal story and brought the message to life. This is the story he told:

If we leverage our own unique strengths, we can have a very bright future even without China.

Many of you know I'm originally Malaysian Chinese, but many may not know that I came to Singapore alone, without my parents, at the age of 12. At that age, I'd learned that the university I wanted to attend after school in Malaysia had limited opportunity for me. People of my origin, Malaysian Chinese, have a quota of only 10 percent of the available places. So, I asked my parents if they could send me to Singapore. My parents said yes, and I came here. I went to a local community school here, nothing flashy. My early days here in the school were challenging. I had just joined the school, and I did not have my uniform yet, but I was allowed to wear my old school uniform.

One day, the discipline master started scolding me in the playground. His voice was getting louder and louder. The crowd around me was growing bigger and bigger. But I was not able to understand anything because, back then, I could hardly speak or understand English. You see, when I moved to Singapore, I was getting by just fine by talking to most of my class in Mandarin. And I spoke in Malay to only a small number. I thought I could get away with not having to make any effort to learn English.

But the scolding from the discipline master was a great reminder that just coming to Singapore wasn't enough. I had to learn English and learn it as fast as I could. The reason why I was being scolded was because I was wearing a belt that was part of my old school uniform but which was not allowed in Singapore schools.

In this moment of discomfort, I looked to my strengths, which were being able to stay resilient when things were tough, finding new ways to adapt, and learning what I needed to learn to stay relevant. This was when I developed a personal core belief: In moments of uncertainty and fear, we can leverage our own unique strengths and can have a very bright future.

I knew I was good with people. So, I started giving Mandarin tutoring to some students. In return, they taught me how to speak English. Before I knew it, I was more than comfortable with the language.

So, if we leverage our own unique strengths, we can have a very bright future.

Now, this personal story does a few things. First, it engages the audience because it shares a lot about their leader that they couldn't have possibly Googled. The leader's story serves as an extremely engaging vehicle to bring the key message to the audience. Imagine this being replaced with the traditional way of opening a strategy deployment, which might run something like this: "I am here to talk about our new strategy which we have worked on post the announcement of China being taken out of our region."

Do you feel the difference?

The story also helps in building an affinity with the leader as it reveals something about the *character* of the speaker. The narrator of the narrative matters, as we have learned in previous chapters.

However, a leader's personal story, while engaging and useful, can be risky if we don't quickly connect it to the organization's change message. After all, the story is about making change happen and not building an affinity with the leader. The next step, then, is to skillfully connect the leader's personal story to the organizational change message.

Step 3: Connect the Leader's Personal Change to the Organizational Change Message

Now is not the time and place to be telling stories for the sake of it. Instead, use a simple statement to connect the leader's personal story to the core change idea of the organization. For example, in the story shared in Step 2 we might create a segue like this:

As you can see, our organization is likewise facing a moment of adversity. It is time for us to find our own unique strengths, too.

Or:

As an organization, we are also facing some difficult moments. It is time for us to leverage our unique strengths.

What the leader is trying to do in Step 3 is to shift people on from the story, which helped people understand the core message with high levels of engagement, to an organizational change message. It is exactly the same message but delivered in a professional way, rather than as a personal one.

To recap, in Step 1 people become clear about the identity they will form as a result of investing energy in making a change happen. In Step 2, they connect with the narrator of the narrative, and in Step 3 the focus is skillfully transitioned from the narrator to the narrative.

From here, it is important to make our employees experience the *need* for change.

Step 4: Get Your Audience to See the Need for Change

There is always some sort of pressure making us change. In *A Beautiful Constraint: How to Transform Your Limitations into Advantages, and Why It's Everyone's Business,* authors Mark Barden and Adam Morgan share a model on how a successful change takes place in an organization, and it is clear that all changes begin with a pressure to change. Visionaries look ahead and plan to act before it is too late to make the change happen. Pressure catalyzes the need to change, and this step is about that pressure. The pressure could be external or internal, or both. To deepen our understanding of this, let's revisit our earlier example of the telecommunications company. Here, the move from a legacy system to a new one in a rapidly changing mobile world was the pressure to change.

To the management, this change was an important step toward the survival of the organization. But, to the people on the ground, it was nothing more than a headache. They were comfortable with the system they were using, so they did not really see the need to learn a new system. Why put in all that effort when what they were doing using the legacy system was just fine? One employee explained how they felt like their fingers were on autopilot with the current system and they didn't need to look at the keyboard. They also said that turning on their various screens in the morning was as natural as getting a coffee. They just walked into the office and launched everything they needed to do their job without having to think at all.

Now, the organization could have just shared all the problems that the old system had and shared what the new system promised. But the biggest issue here was the inefficiency of the old system, which didn't bother the employees. In fact, they were not even aware there was a problem with the old ways of working. So sharing this problem would have no effect. The chances of success would, however, be much bigger if they took a step back and shared what had changed in its world to create the pressure to change.

To help the telecommunication company make its people understand the need for the change, I started sharing an illustration I had designed to show them what had changed in their world (see Figure 19.2 below).

Figure 19.2 How things have changed

The point I highlighted with this visual was that 20 years ago telecommunications had fulfilled very simple needs—for example calling your friends to arrange a meal out—but that today it is one of the most advanced industries in the world: We literally live our life via our telecommunication devices. And so, to keep up with this change, the organization had had to evolve its team support from five to ten departments in two decades. However, the system they worked on was still 20 years old: A system originally designed to cater to basic needs had been enhanced to its maximum capacity to meet the new needs, but could not be enhanced any longer. And as a result employees had to work harder than they should do—tasks that could be taken over by the new system.

After explaining this, I asked the employees: "What do you think? Does the system need to change?"

The moment I put this in front of the teams, they saw the need to make the change effort.

It's time to take a pledge for this chapter.

I pledge to remember and apply following lessons:

- Step 1: Provide your listeners with a new identity that they desire.
- Step 2: Engage your audience with a leader's personal story.
- Step 3: Connect the leader's personal change to the organizational change message.
- Step 4: Get your audience to see the need for change.

Let's look at a few more of the steps of the maximal narrative.

CHAPTER 20

Assembling a Maximal Narrative

PART 2

● ● ●

Estimated reading time: 12 minutes

Narratives have a structure that makes them stick.

(For a visual guide to all ten steps, please refer to Figure 19.1.)

Step 5: Provide a Story of Someone Negatively Impacted by the Problem

The whole point of a strategic corporate narrative is to make a change happen by moving people in the right direction. Individual stories are a great way to move people because they resonate with them.

For example, Sally works for a leading telecommunications company as a direct salesperson. Her role is door-to-door selling. The company she works for is implementing a change in IT systems. Sally has heard her managers give the usual reason-filled "why we need to change" presentation several times. Does she care? Well, we all know the answer to that by now!

However, Sally does care about something else, which is making her life easier. If changing the IT system can make this happen, then she will be motivated to be a part of the change. Here is a story Sally shares about her frustration with the way things are:

A couple of days ago, I was trying to pitch to an old lady. We were probably taking a bit too long for her because we needed to use the system to check her particulars, and it was taking a long time to get the information we needed. She wanted to go home and prepare dinner, but we had to keep her for longer because of the slow system. The lady wasn't pleased, and I didn't really feel proud about my work.

Now, if we had a new IT system, we could make a promise to change this story:

A couple of days ago, I was trying to pitch to an old lady. She informed me she was in a rush and only had a few minutes. I took her details and processed the information in the system, and she was done within less than a quarter of an hour. She was happy she could renew her mobile subscription and get back home to cook on time. Seeing her happy made me very proud of the work I do.

In essence, if a change manages to show a bright future for those who need to exert the energy to make the change happen, it is a change people find worth being a part of. People are willing to work hard to make the change happen, but only if they find it meaningful for themselves. Generic reasons like "We are changing to gain market share" says nothing to them—and why should it?

We tend to rely on giving people knowledge about the problem we are aiming to solve. But people don't act when they've been given knowledge about a problem; they act when they *feel* the problem and gain an understanding. One of my personal experiences should bring this contention home:

"Please turn on TunnelBear [a secure VPN service] when you travel overseas and use hotel Wi-Fi." This is what a well-wisher had been telling me for years, and I'd always had a standard response to this advice, "Yes," but the truth was, I'd never turned TunnelBear on because it just seemed like an effort for no real gain. Didn't the whole world use hotel Wi-Fi? There was nothing wrong with it.

However, a few years ago something happened to challenge my assumption. I watched a movie (a form of storytelling!) based on real-life incidents in which there were scenes of a young women's laptop camera being used to watch her in her hotel. That challenged my assumption about the security of hotel Wi-Fi. Every time I am in a hotel room now, that scenes plays out in front of my eyes. This led to me to change my behavior, and now I always turn TunnelBear on. Storytelling had shown me that what I was doing was wrong.

My initial view of not finding anything wrong with what I was doing is no different from those employees in an organization who do not jump and embrace change, but, on the contrary, question it. So, unless we demonstrate to employees how what they are doing is wrong, we won't be able to initiate the change—just as the movie had demonstrated to me that my careless behavior by not turning TunnelBear on was wrong.

Most of us are like that fish in the water which when asked, "How is the water?" responds by saying, "What *is* water?" The fish doesn't know it lives in water. I didn't understand the consequences of not using TunnelBear, and our employees don't understand the need for change when you merely ask them to change.

For this step, you will have to adopt an identity of a reflective or journalist storyteller to find the story and then that of a reporter to shape the story so you can tell in a compelling manner. You need to remember, too, that this story is only a part of the overall narrative.

At this point in your narrative, you will most likely have the more skeptical people in the audience saying to you, "This is anecdotal, based only on a story of an individual or on your personal experience." So now it's time to add magnitude by adding data to support the story. Let's move on to Step 6.

Step 6: Add Data to Establish the Magnitude of the Problem

Many people have the entrenched view that every storyteller, whether fictional or corporate, just wants their audience to "get drunk" on emotions, so they lose track of any rational considerations and yield to the teller's agenda. They'll say that you suspend disbelief when you hear a story.

In a professional setting, this notion works against the storyteller, so, it's best to add data to show the magnitude of the problem you are trying to solve. One of my favorite ways to connect the story to the supporting data is to add the phrase "And the numbers tell exactly the same story."

For example, if in Step 5 you have shared a story of an individual like Sally, now you need to tell us that many more Sallys exist and how this affects the organization's overall performance.

Let's use the example of Sheryl Sandberg's very famous 2010 TED Talk "Why we have too few women leaders." Sandberg makes a very clear assertion in the first minute of the talk: "Women are not making it to the top of any profession anywhere in the world." Now, before anyone can object, "Ah, but that's just her bias ..." she adds a whole string of data:

> *The numbers tell the story quite clearly. Of 190 heads of state—nine are women. Of all the people in parliament in the world, 13 percent are women. In the corporate sector, women at the top, C-level jobs, board seats—top out at 15, 16 percent. The numbers have not moved since 2002 and are going in the wrong direction. Even in the nonprofit world, a world we sometimes think of as being led by more women, women at the top: 20 percent.*

You can see just how brilliantly Sandberg has managed this transition from a simple assertion to backing it up with data. Just like assertions need data to back them up, so, too, do stories.

If the data is so important, then, why share the story first? Because as Dr. Jill Bolte Taylor—American neuroanatomist, author, and inspirational public speaker—says, "Although many of us may think of ourselves as thinking creatures that feel, biologically we are feeling creatures that think." So, it is always best to make us feel with the story first and then make us think after. And providing data is a very good way to make people think.

Once you're at this stage, people are more likely willing to change because the story has already connected with their heart and the data is now satisfying the needs of their brains. You have induced the motivation in them to want to change.

Step 7: Put in Place Change Assistance

We've now reached a crucial point in the development of your narrative: If you don't provide clear *change assistance* now—something that clearly defines the action your audience needs to take—you run the risk of letting all the motivation built in them to change go to waste. Now is a perfect time to introduce change assistance. This is your clear plan to help people change, not because they *have to* change, but because they *want* to change.

Last year, I helped a client deliver a change narrative for a digital transformation project. We had a solid narrative in place that gave me the confidence we would be able to instill in our audiences the desire to want to change. However, I knew that, if we did not provide clear and manageable change assistance, the desire would dissolve. Manageable because, when something appears manageable, skepticism reduces. For example, one change narrative development that I was involved in had at its core that everyone would use AI-led project management, but toward the end of the narrative, we asked people to sign up to an AI roadshow where there were a lot of workshops to learn about AI.

In a corporate setting, it is advisable to ask for the smallest change possible first, where the stakes are not high, and then move incrementally toward the overall change. Desired changes rarely take place when you present *only* the consequences of not changing or *only* the benefits of changing. Showing people clearly the steps they can take to change, starting with the smallest step, is equally important.

Robert Cialdini, in his book *Pre-Suasion*, suggests that we follow the following rule: Alarming messages about the consequences of bad health habits are more effective than messages about the benefits of good habits. The more attention-grabbing the appeal to your audience's fears is, the more effective will be its power to produce behavior change. Cialdini cites the example of smoking where frightening images on cigarettes pack grab the smoker's attention and create fear.

That said, the most interesting thing about using fear-provoking messages alone is that, even though they succeed in getting attention, they don't fully succeed in mobilizing the desired change. Research has shown that creating high levels of fear in smokers can make them deny they themselves will ever encounter a health issue personally. Denial is a way for an individual to deal with the now-heightened fears and anxiety.

Interestingly, there is a way to deal with this fear—by providing change assistance in which the negative consequences are paired with assistance on how to change.

Frightening message + Change assistance = Change mobilized (Negative Story)

We've already seen how telling a negative story can be useful in narrative, but now by adding change assistance we can mobilize change. For example, imagine you want your team to change the way they do presentations. First, you tell a story about someone who's not good at presenting and the negative consequences this person had to face due to the deficiency. Straight after you have told the story, you provide change assistance by offering to sign them up for a workshop in which they'll be able to learn how to present better.

After you have provided change assistance, the best thing you can do is to show how the person who was previously suffering negative consequences is no longer suffering them.

Step 8: Show How Your Change-Assistance will Help the Suffering Individual

After you have introduced change assistance, next you show how the person's life will change, shifting from negative to positive, with the help of your change assistance. As we saw in Chapter 10, in 2010 Steve Jobs introduced the iCloud strategy at the Worldwide Developers Conference in San Francisco. In one section of this milestone speech, he clearly established the importance of showing how someone's life would change after change assistance. I have paraphrased his speech here:

The devices have changed from how they used to be. In the past, most devices had a single function but now devices are multifunctional: They all have music, they all have photos, they all have videos. At the moment, if I buy and download a song on my iPhone, and I want to get the song to my other devices like my iPad, I have to sync my iPhone to my Mac. If I want to view some photos that are stored on my Mac on my iPhone, I have to sync the two devices. Keeping everything in sync is driving me crazy!

Jobs then went on to present the change assistance he had in mind:

We have a great solution for this problem that's driving us crazy. We think the solution is our next big insight: We're going to move the digital hub, the center of your digital life, into the cloud. Because all these new devices have communications built into them, so they can all talk to the cloud whenever they want.

Finally, he showed how a person's life would be changed after the change assistance:

So now if I download something on my iPhone, it is sent up to the cloud immediately. Let's say I take some pictures on my iPhone. Those pictures are in the cloud, and they are now pushed down to my device automatically.

Now everything's in sync, and I don't even having to think about it. I don't even have to take the devices out of my pocket. I don't have to be near my Mac or PC.

When we show the person's life changing in a positive direction, it takes us to an imaginary future we want to belong to.

Step 9: Show What the Future Holds

In this step, you show what the future looks like after the change has happened. This is not about the individual's future alone but also about the organization's future. There is a combined success in which the organization is succeeding and so is the individual. Examples of such futures might include:

- continuing to be the best workforce in the life sciences
- affording the lifestyle we aspire to
- becoming trusted advisors
- being called key opinion leaders
- winning awards, bonuses, and so on.

The most important thing to keep in mind here is you can't have too much detail in the story at this stage, simply because the future hasn't happened yet! Too many details here run the risk of sounding fake. What's more, the chain of cause and effect must be short: You must show a future that is possible in the near future and not too far away.

At this point in the story, you may find yourself facing objections, questions, or entrenched views. Questions can be useful because they can give you the opportunity to clarify your narrative, but objections and entrenched views are harder to counter and can be an obstacle to successful change implementation.

The next step, the tenth, is about being able to anticipate these roadblocks.

But before that we must take our pledge.

I pledge to remember and apply following lessons:

- Step 5: Provide a story of someone negatively impacted by the problem.
- Step 6: Add data to establish the magnitude of the problem.
- Step 7: Put in place change assistance.
- Step 8: Show how your change assistance will help the individual.
- Step 9: Show what the future holds.

So let's now move on to Step 10, on addressing premade stories.

CHAPTER 21

Assembling a Maximal Narrative

PART 3

● ● ●

Estimated reading time: 10 minutes

Before your audience listen to your story, they already have a premade story they are telling themselves.

(For a visual guide to all ten steps, please refer to Figure 19.1.)

Step 10: Address Premade Stories

Audiences don't come to you as a blank slate. They have their own stories that inform the way they receive your story. I like to call these *premade stories*. Most of the time, we don't know what these premade stories are, and even when we do, our tendency is to just ignore them and get on with the business of telling our audience what we want them to know and do. Mostly, we prefer to talk rather than listen.

This is a mistake, however, because these premade stories can morph into little poisonous mushrooms that speedily grow in the minds of our audience as they listen to us. They tend to be of three types:

- simple objections/questions
- incorrect ingrained views
- correct ingrained views.

As we build our strategic corporate narratives, we need to actively seek out these premade stories. We want to uncover the stories lying just beneath the surface. We want to know what we are dealing with. If these stories are not addressed in advance, no matter what you say, it won't work. These poisonous mushrooms will keep on surfacing.

PREMADE STORY TYPE 1: SIMPLE OBJECTIONS/QUESTIONS

Many years ago, a pharmaceutical company was setting up a plant and asked five companies, including mine, to work on a bid to put together a plant opening experience story, with each given a 30-minute timeslot to present. We knew from the onset that the "Here's our experience" approach was not going to win us this pitch; we needed to do something different. There was a boardroom with close to 20 people from the client's side in it. We looked at the schedule for the day and realized that we had the last slot of the day. By the time it would be our turn, everyone would be fed up with listening to the presentations and any enthusiasm for asking questions would have died.

To counter this, we decided to develop a list of questions the audience might have but would not ask, most likely due to the cognitive overload they would be experiencing from all the other presentations. One of the things we often fail to recognize is that asking questions can be hard, too. So, as a presenter, it is our job to preempt and respond to those questions or any premade stories.

So, on the day, we did a highly visual ten-minute presentation, and then aligned with the client's mental state by saying that we would spend the rest of our slot answering questions we anticipated they had but suspected they wouldn't ask, such as:

- Where did we get the data that supported our story from or what is the source of our data?

- What if the scope of work increases but the budget is set?

- How many people will be in a team if we are awarded the project?

- Do we have experience in handling projects of such nature?

And the list continued for the next 20 minutes. Our list of questions was a simple set of questions we would have liked answered if someone was presenting to us.

And yes, on the way back from the client's office the same day, we did get a call to let us know we has been awarded the project. Sometimes it's not the core idea but a response to your audience's premade stories that will help you win the game.

PREMADE STORY TYPE 2: INCORRECT INGRAINED VIEWS: BELIEFS-BASED

Here we are dealing with premade stories that are incorrect. We may often be tempted to say, "You're wrong in thinking that," but this only reinforces what the person thinks. People believe what they believe and telling them they are wrong is giving them one more reason to reinforce their existing belief. Stories are a great way to help them get rid of incorrect ingrained views. Let's take a look at an example and how a leader was able to deal with such views.

A senior business leader who is known to be a tough, results-driven taskmaster is taking over a new team. This leader has a clear idea of how to transform the new team into a high-performing team. She writes a set of clear key messages and is keen to tell the vision story to the team. But no matter how smart this leader is, and how strategic these key messages are, the team will not perform.

Why?

Because there's an elephant in the room, or, in other words, the team is telling themselves stories like:

- "Oh no, I am going to have to report to this tough taskmaster!"
- "It's so hard working with her."
- "She is so demanding."
- "How I wish I was in the team going to work under a different leadership!"

The newly appointed leader can only be successful in conveying her key messages if she first addresses these stories the team members are telling themselves. The best way to address them would be to tell a story of someone who is just like the audience. Here is a story a leader might tell before telling them her vision:

I want to talk to you about two people whose examples can confirm the way I work with people. Although I'm a tough taskmaster, that's only half the story.

A few years ago, I took over a marketing team which was new to me. When I took over the team, I conducted one-on-one sessions with each of the team members. Those sessions allowed me to get to know Sam and Matt.

Sam is now a senior director, but back then he was a junior manager. I have this vivid memory of being in a conversation with him and he mentioned how keen and passionate he was and how he wanted to do more. Just by speaking up, Sam catalyzed a great career for himself. In the months that followed, Sam worked on some of the best projects and now he is one of the best marketers we have in our organization. He did not get there by being scared, shy, and fearful of a demanding leadership. He got there by speaking up and wanting to work on the best projects.

The other person I want to tell you about is Matt. Whereas Sam was keen to do more, Matt had a different aspiration—he wanted to find the most efficient ways to get the tasks he had at hand done. What was special about Matt was this: No matter what you tasked him with, he got it done in the shortest and most effective way. He had great people skills and knew how to work with the management, too. He really was an organization-savvy type. It took me a while to notice but he had a style of working with me, too. He was aware that finding time with me for necessary approvals was never easy, so, he had a very special routine which was to do all his prep in the morning, catch me at lunchtime, get my approval, get everything done, and leave work at 5 p.m. I noticed his street smartness and so I gave him complex projects.

The point I am making is, if you have a special skill like Matt who was able to navigate the management and other stakeholders, all the best work in this team awaits you. Look at Matt now. He is handling all the major projects, and, in my view, he is one of the best marketers we have. Whether you want to do a lot more like Sam or find ways to work efficiently like Matt, we have a place for you here.

It's my job to find the best in you and set you up for success like I did for Sam and Matt, but it also requires commitment from you. So, yes, I am a tough taskmaster but also someone who is waiting to build amazing careers for you. And this is the complete story.

Rather than jumping to key messages and vision statements straightaway, this leader practiced strategic storytelling and told a story of other team members who have been successful under her leadership, even though she was a tough taskmaster. She removed the premade story before it could spread like those poisonous mushrooms.

In building a strategic corporate narrative, it's advisable for you to list the incorrect ingrained views your audience might have and address them in advance. If, for example, you know that things running your through audience's minds are thoughts like:

- "The price is too high."
- "This is no different from what I am getting from X.":
- "I don't think this really addresses what I need."

use sentences like:

- *"Another client of ours once asked* why the price is so high."
- *"You may think* this is exactly what company X offers."
- *"I'm sure you are wondering* if this really addresses what you want."

and then use stories to overcome these objections.

PREMADE STORY TYPE 3: CORRECT INGRAINED VIEWS: EVIDENCE-BASED

These are not premade stories, but things that have happened which can become a poisonous mushroom if not addressed.

I recently worked on a narrative for the launch of an AI-led project in an organization. I learned there were many people in the company who were frustrated about the launch. The company had already tried the same thing before, but the project had failed miserably. The first thing we did therefore was to acknowledge this failure and share with the team what learning we had gained from the failure. We also insisted that we were not going to repeat the mistake.

So why mention a previous failure?

Because if we do not acknowledge the failure, and prevent it from getting any traction, it risks becoming the subject of gossip during the morning tea break. Before it becomes someone else's gossip, it is best to own it. Owning it takes the power away from the corridor gossips and prevents a past event becoming poisonous.

Of course, it's not enough to just own failures; you have to show the changes you made as a result of them, that you were able to learn from your mistakes. Here is a simple pattern:

- Acknowledge the failure, with self-deprecating humor, if possible. This reduces tension.
- Talk about the lessons learned.
- Show how these lessons have been applied to make a change happen.

Here, finally, is a handy checklist for premade stories:

1	What are the stories your audience are telling themselves?	☐
2	Acknowledge the stories the audience are telling themselves.	☐
3	If these premade stories are simply the questions the audience have, don't wait for the audience to ask them. Answer the questions preemptively and show that you know your audience.	☐
4	If the premade stories are true, acknowledge them and let your audience know what you have learned through the process and how you are applying the lessons.	☐
5	If they aren't true, don't say, "That's not true." Instead, tell your audience a story of someone just like them that they can use as a proxy.	☐
6	The story you choose to tell should be about someone your audience can speak to and find out whether the story or its details are true.	☐

Now we have learned about how to assemble a maximal narrative, it's time for us to turn to the minimal narrative. But first we have to take a pledge.

I pledge to remember and apply the following lessons from Chapter 19, 20, and 21:

- Step 1: Provide your listeners with a new identity that they desire.
- Step 2: Engage your audience with a leader's personal story.
- Step 3: Connect the leader's personal change to the organizational change message.
- Step 4: Get your audience to see the need for change.
- Step 5: Provide a story of someone negatively impacted by the problem.

- Step 6: Add data to establish the magnitude of the problem.
- Step 7: Put in place change assistance.
- Step 8: Show how your change assistance will help the individual.
- Step 9: Show what the future holds.
- Step 10: Address premade stories.

So now let's move on to how to assemble a minimal narrative, where, as you might guess, there are fewer steps!

CHAPTER 22

Assembling a Minimal Narrative

• • •

Estimated reading time: 10 minutes

Minimal is effective because that's all your audience needs.

In the minimal narrative structure there just four steps. It's not a completely new structure but one derived from the maximal narrative structure we looked at in the previous chapter.

Step 1: Nudge Your Audience Toward a New Identity, or State the Point to Motivate Change

This is exactly like Step 1 of the maximal narrative structure: An invitation to adopt a new identity. The point of the narrative is to provide a nudge toward a new identity.

Step 2: Share a Negative Story Where Change Was Not Implemented and the Result

This is like Step 5 of the maximal narrative structure. However, there the point was to demonstrate to the audience what they are doing is wrong because they are unaware of it, while here the goal is to instill in people the desire to change.

Figure 22.1 The minimal narrative

To explore this more deeply, let's first look at some common communications we hear:

- "Our head of sales, Natalie, is excellent. I wish everyone was like her."
- "Mariam is top of class in her grades. I hope all students can become like her."
- "Sandy is a great writer; she always comes up with the best articles. I wish everyone could write like her."

What do these statements have in common? These express the hopes of someone who wants a change for the better. Often, the speaker of such statements—a manager, a teacher, or a parent—says these things in the hope of sharing success stories and creating role models that inspire others. However, this way of communicating rarely achieves the desired outcome of everyone becoming like Natalie, Mariam, and Sandy.

Why?

Let's try to understand this by using an example taken from the iconic children's TV series *Sesame Street*. This show debuted in 1969 with the express purpose of using stories to educate and influence pre-schoolers. The program has been so successful that Elmo, Big Bird, and Cookie Monster continue to enthrall, influence, and educate more than 170 million children in 140 countries.

When the creators of *Sesame Street* wanted to help kids learn how to pay attention to and control their impulses, they decided to use the character Cookie Monster—who, of course, can't resist cookies—as their example. They realized that children needed to see someone struggling with the same issues they were struggling with, and trying out multiple techniques to overcome them.

Now, this is exactly what's missing from the statements like those above. We are so focused on the others' success that we miss out telling the most important thing: What exactly did Natalie, Mariam and Sandy do to be good at what they do? What were their struggles, and how did they overcome them?

Effective storytelling happens when we tell our audience about some-one who is struggling like them, not when we cite examples of successful individuals. The adversity shared in the telling is the crux of resonance where the people who are listening gasp and say, "She sounds just like me!" Resonance comes from articulating the problem.

Before we move on to Steps 3 and 4, let's look at an example of assembling a minimal narrative focusing especially on Steps 1 and 2.

Adam works as the head of corporate communications in a hospital. He is about to announce a new initiative to the entire hospital, the for-mation of a Pediatric Rapid Response Initiative.

In the usual hospital setting, escalating care for a deteriorating patient is mostly a hierarchical process. The nurses inform the ward doctors, who then review the patient and may, in turn, get a more senior doctor to review the case as well. Only then is the patient transferred to inten-sive care, if required. This all takes time, which, when a child's health is deteriorating, is crucial. The Pediatric Rapid Response Initiative is a process in which, when the first signs of deterioration are noticed, any hospital staff or particularly parents (who may not know exactly what's wrong with their child but do know that *something* is wrong) are able to urgently inform a specialized team of doctors and nurses, who will arrive at the ward and give immediate attention to the patient.

The desired outcome from Adam's presentation is that everyone will approve of the initiative and work toward making it successful. But would Adam get the support he is looking for if he was simply to announce the change? Probably not, because he is asking people to stop doing what they know and have always been doing, and to start doing something new, with risk control being taken away from them. There would be worries like:

- "Why change something that seems to be working well?"
- "The rapid response team would take over my patient and we would lose control over the care of the patient."
- "Parents or relatives would have the ability to circumvent our authority. They may misuse the ability to call in another team."

Does this sound familiar? Before you can drive the desired change, you have so much resistance to overcome. A negative story can be of great help in such a situation. Here is what I would suggest Adam do to successfully introduce the change.

Adam's need is to stimulate a desire for action, but if he doesn't have the audience's attention, his story will fall on deaf ears. To get attention, you need to tell a story about failure. Rivet the audience with a story and kill the little voice in their heads saying, "I have emails building up. I must get to my next clinic. This is just more administrative nonsense, and I need to get out of here." But before he gives them this negative story, Adam first needs to give his audience a nudge toward a new identity or state the point to make a change. This is Step 1.

Today I want to talk about us as healthcare professionals who save lives, and it doesn't matter if we do that ourselves or are a part of the ecosystem that saves lives. The point is saving lives is way more important than guarding our identities as people who only through their own actions can save lives. Sometimes we have to help others save lives and that's also saving lives."

Next, Adam needs to share a story of a person who has been negatively impacted (the failure/negative story). This is Step 2.

Adam could use as his failure story a real-life example from a hospital in the USA. Josie King was admitted to the hospital after suffering severe burns from climbing into a hot bath. She had healed and was set to return home two weeks later, but Josie died days before she was to be released. She had an undetected CVC infection and severe dehydration.

164

After Josie left the pediatric intensive care unit (PICU), her central venous catheter (CVC) was removed. Every time the toddler saw a drink, she screamed for it. She was sucking feverishly at her washcloth. Josie's mother asked the nurses about this and was assured it was normal. It was not something Josie had ever done before. Josie's mother had been with her daughter every minute from the day she entered the hospital. The nurses assured her that Josie was doing well, and suggested it was time for her to go and get some sleep at home.

Arriving back at the hospital at 5 a.m., Josie's mother knew something was drastically wrong. The medical team was called. They administered naloxone, and Josie's mom asked if she could give her daughter something to drink. Josie gulped down a liter of juice. Verbal orders were given: no more narcotics. Josie began to seem a little better.

At 1 p.m., a nurse came with a syringe of methadone. Josie's mother told her there was an order for no narcotics. The nurse responded that the order had been changed. She gave Josie the injection. Soon after, Josie's heart stopped. Her mother was ushered out of the room.

The next time Josie's mother saw her daughter, it was back on the PICU floor. Her child was hooked up to lots of monitors and looked awful. Eighteen-month-old Josie King died in her mother's arms two days later. She had a hospital-acquired infection, was severely dehydrated, and had been given inappropriate narcotics.

This story will grab people's attention; they'll feel the pain and, as medical professionals, will feel responsibility for what's happened. On the other hand, it will leave them in the lurch, not knowing what to do next. At this stage of your minimal narrative, you have your audience yearning to change the situation, so now is the perfect time to give a solution.

Step 3: Tell a Success/Positive Story

This is the most crucial step of your narrative—the one that sparks the desire to change. Let's return to the Pediatric Rapid Response Initiative. An imagined success story Adam could create might be as follows:

Sixteen-month-old Logan was admitted to the emergency department. Logan had problems breathing, and the doctors had advised his parents to keep him in the hospital to be monitored. Overnight, Logan's health started deteriorating. His heart rate and respiratory rate were very high. At 4 a.m.

(a time at which staffing is low, staff are tired and overworked, and the risk of something going wrong increases), Logan's mother, Angel, informed the nurse about Logan's change.

Instead of the usual hierarchical method of escalating the care, the Pediatric Rapid Response Team was called in to stabilize Logan. An immediate decision was made to take Logan to the ICU. Logan was stabilized and saved by immediate action based on the initial signs. But imagine if we had followed the same old protocol—would Logan have still been OK?

What is most important here is that you are issuing an invitation to imagine an outcome, but not concluding anything for your audience. It's up to your audience to make the decision. But by using the two contrasting stories, you have first captured their attention, and then shown them the positive benefits of the desired change.

Step 4: Invite Your Audience to Make Their Own Mind Up on What Is the Future They See for Themselves

Motivating people to want to change is important, but not enough. The desire to change may wear off unless we provide reinforcing facts to support our idea for change. In Adam's case, the facts he could use could come from data from a different hospital, for example a report that 2012 was a cardiac arrest-free year due to its Pediatric Rapid Response Team's efforts.

Adam concludes his presentation by stating that he has painted two pictures in front of the audiences today. One of Josie and another of Logan and we have to make a choice where we belong.

Building and Releasing Tension

The minimal narrative structure outlined above has often been used in famous speeches given by world leaders, as US speaker and CEO Nancy Duarte has shared. According to Duarte, in great speeches, the speaker builds tension and releases it, and builds tension and releases it again. To achieve this tension and release, you must get to a place of shared understanding by stating what everyone knows to be true. If you're giving a presentation to the rest of your sales or marketing team, this could be as simple as saying, "Uh oh, we're not performing well this quarter." Here you build your credibility because you show that you understand "what is." Next, you want to introduce "what could be." This is the first time your audience will have reached a heightened sense of cathartic tension as you're asking for today's realities to be different.

What I am calling a negative story, Duarte is referring to as a "what is"—the grim reality of today that needs to change. And her "what could be" is the positive story eliciting desire.

Now you have learned both narratives structures, it's time for us to look at some real case studies where these narratives come to life. But, before that, let's take a pledge.

I pledge to remember and apply the following lessons:

- Step 1: Nudge your audience toward a new identity, or state the point to motivate change
- Step 2: Share a story of a person who has been negatively impacted.
- Step 3: Share a success/positive story.
- Step 4: Invite your audience to make their own mind up on what is the future they see for themselves.

In the next chapter, our first case study of constructing strategic corporative narratives will relate to something we are all facing—digital transformation.

CHAPTER 23

Strategic Corporate Narratives for Digital Transformation

* * *

Estimated reading time: 17 minutes

The catalyst to digital adoption is a narrative.

My work took something of a special turn in 2016. I found myself spending more time in factories, plants, and call centers than on stage giving keynotes or in office buildings teaching people how to tell stories in a corporate setting. I found myself more in sneakers than in heels. More in bunny suits than in dresses. More in hard hats than with nicely blow-dried hair.

I realized that the demand for my work was coming more from environments that were digitally transforming. Digital transformation was the most in-demand narrative with which I was helping organizations from 2016 onwards.

That same year, a large telecommunications company asked me to help curate a story for a digital transformation project they were working on. They needed to change from a 20-year-old legacy system to a new age customer relationship management (CRM) system. I've mentioned this project a few times before in the book but not in its entirety. In this chapter, I'll take you through each step of the narrative I helped this organization to develop.

Before I begin, let me explain what I mean by *digital transformation*.

What Is Digital Transformation?

Early in 2022, I worked with the Global Head Third-Party Security Risk at a leading bank. Her job involves making sure every digital vendor that the bank brings on board is verified. She leads a team of ten, and they are all cyber security professionals. In 2019, her small team of ten delivered 1,900 digital vendor verifications, which was already a lot for them since most of the work was manual. Then came the year 2020 where digital ways of working became more prominent due to the impact of COVID-19, and without any warning her team was tasked to do 2,200 verifications. Her team was already stretched, but they had no choice and had to deliver. In 2021, her team was told to expect at least 4,200 vendor verifications. Two thoughts might be running through your mind right now: Why did the numbers go so crazy? Would it even be possible to meet the new demands? Let's answer both these questions.

First, why did the numbers go so crazy? After COVID-19, the bank needed multiple digital vendors to support single functions. Take, for example, video conferencing services for meetings. In the current digitally transformed world, you need not just one but three approved vendors. In the past, video conferencing was a secondary solution, but during the COVID-19 pandemic it became primary. Therefore, the team needed to work on a lot more vendor verifications in 2021. COVID-19 created the pressure to change.

At time of writing, and as things return to a new normal, video conferencing remains important. Video conferencing will never be a secondary solution again. If anything, an evolved and enhanced version of digital meetings, like meetings in the metaverse, is what the future holds.

Next question: Would it even be possible to meet the new demands? The answer is yes but only by using digital tools that assist with vendor verifications. Many companies are shifting from manual labor-based organizations to digital-transformed organizations to remove the manual effort on non-value work. This team was able to achieve the spiraling number of vendor verifications because they became a digitally transformed organization.

This is a classic example of digital transformation—using new, fast, and frequently changing digital technology to solve problems. The problems are mostly centered around reliance on manual labor, productivity, and efficiency, which eventually lead to plummeting profitability.

I live in Singapore, and even during the COVID-19 crisis digital transformation played a key role. In May 2020, a four-legged robot started patrolling a park in Singapore to remind people of safe distancing measures. Named Spot, the robot assists with safe distancing efforts in parks, gardens, and nature reserves by broadcasting a recorded message. Spot is fitted with cameras and uses video analytics to help it estimate the number of visitors in each park where it operates. Now imagine if we had to get humans to do the same job: It would be an extremely complex process, involving both staffing and risk issues.

Technology is removing the inherent issues of managing people and getting work done at large scale. And that is a huge component of digital transformation. In organizations, its enablers are robotics, automation, cloud computing, and so on.

Narratives for Digital Transformation

Now you know what digital transformation is, let's look at why narratives are needed for success with digital transformation.

There is no argument about the fact that digital transformation comes with a promising future story. Its potential is limitless, so we can't avoid it and must learn to befriend it. But it is also our responsibility to show people how to embrace it and not fear it. Employees typically respond to these changes in the following manner:

- "OMG, I've got to learn all this new technology!"
- "I think I am going to get pushed out."
- "Bosses only care about profitability and not people."
- "My career is over: The machines have taken over!"

This situation is akin to army commanders knowing why a war is important but the soldiers who have to fight the war on the front line not believing in the war. The result: The commanders will find it hard to get the soldiers onto the battlefield, and even if they do, they won't fight with the enthusiasm required to win in a battle. By contrast, if soldiers hear their leaders telling them *why* they are fighting the war, they get an adrenaline rush that's so big they just want to go out and win the war.

A good narrative can have the same effect, creating an adrenaline rush where people want to embrace the transformation. The seed of digital transformation that needs to be planted using a narrative is well explained by Cal Newport, author of *Deep Work*. Newport shares that the person who learns to work with machines will see success in the twenty-first century and beyond. Technology gives us efficiency, but adoption of the technology is dependent on human desire, and an integration of the two is where success resides.

The three stages of change, as is well known, are storming, norming, and performing. As we are still at the "storming" stage of understanding this technology-led change, we need narratives to bring meaning and scale up adoption. In such a situation, it becomes the leader's role to show the path promising the individual personal success. Why? Because, almost invariably, companies trying to embrace digital change fall down not on sourcing it but on getting people to adopt it.

If you can't tell a good digital transformation narrative, you won't be able to get people to integrate well with the technology. They'll fight it. All the gains you're trying to get with the technology you'll lose because people will resist. A leader has to address the fears associated with technology and bring people round to Marie Curie's point of view: "Nothing in life is to be feared, it is only to be understood. Now is the time to understand more, so we may fear less."

This chapter shows you ways to make others understand the need for digital transformation. A client—Francis—and I were having a conversation about the digital transformation. He heads the supply chain function of a large multinational corporation. I asked him, "What do you fear the most about this transformation?" His response was: "Bringing people along the journey of this transformation."

I wasn't surprised by Francis' answer, because every leader I know would have given the same response. But I'm an optimist: Humans are far more complex than any technology, but, unlike an algorithm, which, once set, performs per instruction, a human can change in nanoseconds. It's this ability to change and adapt frequently that gives humans the capacity to persuade and influence others to change, and narrative is your tool to do this.

Let me show you how it can be—and has been—done.

A CASE STUDY OF DIGITAL TRANSFORMATION

A company was introducing a new CRM system. There were 10,000 employees in the organization. The current system was a legacy system, having been put in place 20 years before, and people were comfortable with working with it—so comfortable, in fact, that they had gradually become habituated to its disadvantages, too.

I was approached by the project lead to help with a story to motivate people to stop using what they have used for years and start using the new system. I clearly remember a comment from a rank-and-file staff member in one of the early meetings: "Turning the current CRM system on and working on it is as normal as waking up and having a coffee for me. Why would I want to change that?" As soon as I heard her comment, I knew that we had an arduous task ahead of us.

It was not simply a matter of introducing a new system but making the people who would use the system say, "I want to use this new system."

Here is how we built our maximal change narrative for digital transformation. As ever, it is important to remember that these steps are a guide, not a rigid rulebook. If you don't need all ten steps, don't use them!

Step 1: Provide Your Listeners with a New Identity

I spoke to the leadership team about how we intended to position this new system. They articulated it as a system that would be future proof, providing enhanced productivity, removing complexity, and fostering collaboration.

Imagine if you were an employee working in this organization's headquarters and, walking along its corridors or going to the canteen, you saw posters promoting the new system in exactly these terms, what would you feel? Would you even feel anything at all? Mostly, you would ignore them.

So, after much thought and discussion, we changed the positioning. This how the leadership started talking about it:

We want all our staff to say, "I can get my job done faster and better. And I am proud of the quality of my work."

We started designing posters that instilled staff with a feeling of efficiency and pride. Staff took notice because it was relevant. This was their new identity. They were already experiencing moments on the ground when, due to the sloppiness of the old system, they were getting frustrated. But because the posters showed them what was possible, they started identifying the feeling *as* frustration. The communication from the leadership team had caught their attention.

Step 2: Engage Your Audience with a Leader's Personal Story

Now before the leadership team could start talking about the new system, they had to build connections with the team, but not just any old connection. They needed connections that would keep the current situation in mind. This connection would build a bond with the speaker—the leader—and increase their chances of being heard. We listen to people we like.

The two most important things to keep in mind at this step are:

- You must share something people can't Google about you.
- You must make people feel you are just like them—commonality, remember, connects.

Here is how a leader could build connection by sharing a personal experience:

I want to start today by sharing with you a moment from my life when I was in a very similar situation as you are all in today. The year was 2010, and I was working as a supervisor with a competitor brand. We were informed of the system change and put through training for a few days before we went live with the new system.

In the training environment, my colleagues and I did fine. And then we went live. When I sat down in front of the new system it was as if I had never *seen it before. I made mistake after mistake. I got scolded by the leaders because even as a supervisor I was not able to get it right. My palms were sweaty, and I could feel the sweat pouring off my brow even in the air-conditioned room.*

174

Step 3: Connect the Leader's Personal Change to the Organizational Change

Now, why am I telling you this? Well, because no matter how much training you go through for the upcoming change in our system, learning to operate a new system is a tacit knowledge. It's knowledge you can only gain by doing the work.

What is important is repetition and doing the task, not listening to lectures. So, when we go live with the new system, make mistakes because each mistake takes you closer to mastering the system. Now some of you may be wondering why we are changing the system, when you think the old system is working just fine. But let me explain ..."

Step 4: Get Your Audience to See the Need for Change

This is the step that aims at getting a physiological reaction from your audience in the form of a gasp or statements like "Oh, I didn't know that."

For the telecommunication company to make people understand the need for change, the leader started by sharing a diagram. I have given this diagram before, but this time I'll provide the exact script the leader used to accompany the diagram:

Figure 23.1 How things have changed

Twenty years ago, when we developed our current system, our industry was meeting a typical need for our consumers, which was the ability to call your friends and arrange to go out for a meal perhaps. Now, our customers' needs have evolved, and our industry fulfills those needs, which include messaging, making payments, engaging with social media, etc.

Now, let's look at how internally we evolved to support those needs. Twenty years ago, we had five departments and now we have eight.

So, over the 20 years, our customers evolved, we evolved, but our system remained the same. As our needs evolved, we would keep adding layers onto our system to make it work. A bit like you adding external attachments to your electronic devices to make them relevant. But we have come to a point where the old system won't work anymore. So, we must change it.

Step 5: Provide a Story of Someone Negatively Impacted by the Problem

In this step, we shared stories about the people who were impacted by the limitations of the current system. Here is just one of the stories we collected from conversations on the ground by wearing our journalist hats:

Our team was brought in to consolidate 13 different systems. There is no consistency among these systems. Every system is managed by a business owner who has his or her own agency of choice. Someone gets one agency to do something; someone else gets another agency to another thing. Just the design could be done by ten different agencies. When they come together, they look like a zoo. We have two different websites representing our company, but both look 80 percent different. I find it very hard to build trust with customers as our representation is all over the place. To be honest, I'm not proud of the work we do.

Step 6: Add Data to Establish the Magnitude of the Problem

In all, we collected 96 stories from eight departments. When we spoke to the people, we highlighted the root cause of these problems is the system. We analyzed the words used by the people and what they were feeling via the stories we collected.

Figure 23.2 Feelings associated with system problems

We then shared the patterns that emerged from the stories. We analyzed the stories and tied them to a key point. Every department had a clear pattern: People weren't feeling good because of the limitations of the system, especially the lack of integration between systems. At this stage, through careful analysis of data and story, we were able to make people *feel* that the system needed to be changed.

They were now ready for the change.

Step 7: Put in Place Change Assistance

Only at this stage did we bring in the new CRM system into the picture. "Our new CRM system is designed to help you," we told our audience, and we provided details about the CRM system.

Step 8: Show How Your Change Assistance Will Help the Individual

During this step, leaders carefully worked through each problem story across the departments and explained how the new system would solve the problem. Here's one example:

A few weeks ago we were at telecommunications and technology exhibition. Our staff were all given a state-of-the art iPad to help with accessing

177

information and signing up visitors for promotional packages, but despite the high staff numbers and the sleek iPads, we had a very low signup. And the reason for that was the time it took to finish one signup—the system was just so slow. The slowness was caused by having to pull the information from no fewer than 36 systems. The speaker then revealed that, with the new system, the information would come from a single place and therefore signup would be much faster. At this stage, we invited all employees to sign up for training on the new CRM system, which, as mentioned before, was a "clear and small" action.

After the core of the narrative had been developed, close to a hundred leaders were taught how to tailor the narrative to their own department's needs. They learned how to engage deeply with their teams through the telling of the narrative, so the teams felt nudged toward the new identity and to act in the right direction.

Step 9: Show What the Future Holds

Here we went back to where we started, sharing a vison of the future in which we would equip staff to be able to get their jobs done faster and better and be proud of the quality of their work.

Step 10: Address Premade Stories

In this section, we anticipated what would go through people's minds and how this could become a barrier to our success. So, we started listing the objections and coming up with responses. Here are some of the objections we responded to:

Premade story: "The bosses will never really know what our frustrations are."

Response: Team leaders and staff will attend the same training. When team leads attend the same training not only do they understand the problems of their team members but they also learn how best to address them.

Premade story: "We will be left to manage on our own working with the new system."

Response: In the immediate days after the new system goes live, hyper-care will be provided. An arrangement has been made to have change agents always present supporting staff and helping them build confidence with the system.

Since 2016, I have worked on close to 20 digital transformation narratives. However, in 2018 I began to curate another type of narrative, which has since become very popular—this is the narrative for diversity, equity, and inclusion in organizations. Before I share more about this, let's take the pledge for this chapter.

I pledge to remember and apply the following lessons:

- Digital transformation narratives are one of the most needed narratives in corporate organizations today.
- Employees in organizations have not yet become comfortable with digital transformation and feel threatened by it. The fear lies in the belief they may be replaced by a robot or automation.
- It is the leader's role to shape and tell narratives to infuse the desire in people to want to change.
- Making the digital transformation narrative relevant so it resonates is key.

Now let's tackle the diversity, equity, and inclusion narratives in organizations.

CHAPTER 24

The Application of Narratives in Diversity, Equity, and Inclusion

• • •

Estimated reading time: 14 minutes

The success of a narrative structure lies in giving people the tools to be efficient, time to reflect, and assistance to build their own narratives confidently

In August 2018, I met a very charismatic leader in the boardroom of his organization's Singapore office. He said, "DEI [diversity, equity, and inclusion] is an important aspect of our growth strategy." This leader was at the head of a team of 4,000 employees in a factory. He clearly articulated to me that diversity wasn't optional because there was a skills shortage in the country. There were, however, challenges.

The three categories of diversity that were helping the organization increase the number of people to the levels required were:

- *Gender diversity:* Getting more women into the workforce
- *Intergenerational diversity:* Getting more recent graduates into the workforce
- *Intercultural diversity:* Getting more foreigners into the workforce.

However, achieving this diversity was something of a challenge because, although all these different types of people were getting employed by the organization, they struggled to work well with one another. They were a team in theory but not in practice.

The Problem with Diversity

The organization had diversity, but this was unhelpful without inclusion—the real catalyst for growth in the diverse working environment. Only when this diverse group of people knew how to work with each other could they reap the benefits of their diversity. Diversity with inclusion is an asset, but without inclusion it is a liability.

We thus had a very clear change we wanted to make in the factory: To get a very homogeneous workforce that had long taken comfort in their similar ways of working to embrace diversity and reap its benefits by including everyone. The message was clear and concise:

We already have diversity, but only if we bring inclusion to our diverse workforce will we benefit from it.

An organization's instinct at this point would be to just go and share this message and hope everyone will change, but the problem with this commonly adopted way of managing change is that the message is too broad. It's too conceptual and confusing, and it leaves people wondering what exactly inclusion means. Of course, anyone can Google what inclusion means, but what does in mean in *their context*? Where exactly is inclusion not being practiced?

In such a scenario, most people would simply nod in agreement and sing the song that inclusion is important, while not really having any understanding of how to change behaviors on the ground and make the desired change happen.

Both the leader of the organization and I agreed that, even though we had a clear, concise, and credible message, we would not be able to make people act in the right direction unless we made the message relevant to them, connecting it to their experience.

So, before we began building our narrative, we adopted the identity of the journalist storyteller and started collecting moments (in the form of stories) where employees could see inclusion *not* being practiced. In this way, we wanted to bring clarity to the rather vague, nebulous message of inclusion.

In what follows, I'll take you through the step-by-step process of how we made inclusion happen in this organization. In this organization, middle-aged, male employees formed the majority group, with the minority groups made up by women, younger employees, and foreign nationals from neighboring countries such as China, Taiwan, Singapore, Korea, etc.

Step 1: Become a Journalist and Find Stories/ Moments Where Inclusion Has Failed

With the help of a translator, I interviewed and collected close to a hundred stories where inclusion had not been practiced. The trick here was to make sharing simple for team members by asking about specific moments:

For minority groups:

- Can you talk to me about a time when you felt frustrated about being a woman engineer?
- When was the last time things were difficult due to the fact that you are a new college graduate?
- Can you share a moment when you really experienced the difficulties of being a foreigner?

For majority groups:

- Give me an example of when you found it challenging to address a female team member.
- Share a moment when a new college graduate surprised you, in a good or bad way.
- Give me an example of a difficult or a pleasant working experience with a foreigner.

Here are some tips to make sure you work effectively as a good journalist storyteller in this area:

- Interview diverse people to ensure you capture all perspectives.
- Typically, don't focus your questions on a single emotion. Avoid asking questions only about difficulties or problems but try to elicit contrasting, more positive emotions, too. In this instance, however, I avoided asking the majority group questions that could be answered either positively or negatively, as culturally the majority group is highly polite: If an option had been presented, they would have shared only good moments in their interactions with their fellow workers, which would have hardly been useful. This leads to my next point.

- Make sure you try to understand the culture of the country and company before you start interviewing. I watched ten local language films and read a few books by local authors. Films and books are a great way to understand a culture. The leader of the organization was also extremely helpful in contextualizing everything for me.

- Try to conduct interviews in casual environments. There's a reason why we hear the most useful stories in cafés and pubs and at dinner parties, and not in corporate boardrooms.

- Record the conversations, making sure you get the person's permission to do so, and warning them not to mention any names. We are interested in *what* happened, not in who did what to whom. There are occasions where this is relevant, but they are rare.

After I had carried out the interviews, the stories were translated into English, transcribed, and sent to me.

Step 2: Clean Your Story Bank

I started reading all the stories and deleting the ones that clearly didn't matter. I also needed to edit out any dialogue in the transcripts that was unimportant to the story being told. Eventually, I was left with a good bank of stories I needed to understand and categorize.

Step 3: Understand the Main Point of Each Story and Categorize it Accordingly

I read every story a few times and tried to understand the main point the story was making. Some stories had very clear points, but others needed to be clarified through further investigation.

For example, one of the stories a foreign employee shared described their having attended a technical orientation conducted only in the local language, even though the attendee was unable to understand the language. I couldn't believe something like this could even take place, so I made further inquiries. It transpired that, while all employees hired in this factory had to be able to have at least a basic proficiency in the local language, some did not have a sufficient command of the language to understand technical specifications of the kind given in the training.

In another story, a female engineer shared a story about being invited to be part of the main team one day and then being taken off the next day with no explanation. Her supervisor later shared how he had quickly realized that the work would involve many late nights and had therefore decided to remove the female engineer from the main team to ensure she could get back home on time. Of course, he had failed to share this motivation with her.

Having got to the bottom of the stories, I labeled each accordingly— for example:

- cultural bias
- training issues
- communication challenges.

I now had a bank of highly engaging stories. At this point, it might have been tempting to try to fix every problem individually, but the result of that would have been to fix no problem at all. Instead, we needed an overall strategy derived from the story data we had collected.

Step 4: Analyze Story Data to Gain Insights

Figure 24.1 shows a sample of the data I collected. (Note that, for reasons of confidentiality, I am unable to share all the data.) When I analyzed the data, it became clear that the biggest challenge was communication. Now the more skeptical among my readers may object: "That's hardly an insight: I mean we're talking about a factory in a country where foreigners have joined the workforce. Of course the language barrier is the biggest challenge!" But this thinking would be biased: When we looked at the stories, the communication issue here was not usually a language barrier but mostly about what was *not* said or *how* things were said. Communication is so much more than just the spoken words.

For example, a male engineer told a female colleague who was working late, "You're working so late. Is your husband OK with this?" The male engineer expressed this as a concern, but the female engineer felt excluded: "Would he have said that to me if I was a male engineer?" On another occasion, a young engineer shared that when they were asked by senior leaders, "When did you graduate from university?" And the young engineer provided the information, the senior leaders would often

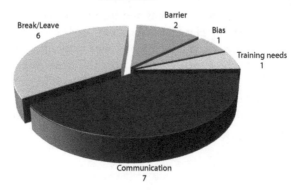

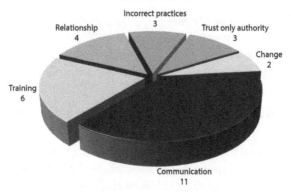

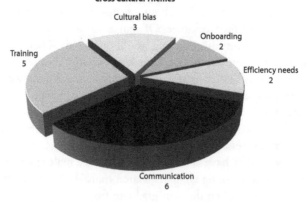

Figure 24.1 Sample data

respond by saying, "Oh you belong to the *that* generation!" (When the leaders said "*that* generation" what they implied was a certain generation who had been through reduced hours and content of the curriculum in primary education.) When leaders respond in that way, the younger generation feels that their scholastic ability is being questioned or undermined. But when you ask the leaders, they say, "I was simply stating a fact and trying to learn how best to work with this younger generation. My intention certainly wasn't to undermine."

We had now reached a stage where we had a clear insight that it was *mis*communication that was the reason behind the lack of inclusion in the diverse workforce. We had refined our point of view and so could build a better change message.

We had started this project with:

We already have diversity, but only if we bring inclusion to this diverse workforce will we benefit from it.

After the analysis of the story-generated data, we refined this to:

We already have diversity, but only if we bring inclusion to this diverse workforce will we benefit from it. And our biggest barrier to inclusion is miscommunication.

We now had a clear, concise, and credible message, but would it connect with the employees and create new behaviors? The answer was clearly no, as we still had to communicate this message to the employees. It was time to move on to Step 4.

Step 5: Demonstrate to the Teams Where Inclusion Is Failing and What the Miscommunication Is

I gave the stories to the team members to read so they could understand each other's perspectives. I wanted them to specifically understand the problems with miscommunication. As the employees read these stories, they became more knowledgeable about the challenge of inclusion and about where and how inclusion breaks down.

Truth be told, no one in this organization was waking up in the morning deciding to be noninclusive, but somehow, again and again, they were falling into noninclusive behaviors. Reading these real stories became a tools for correcting their behavior.

Could we have just left things there and hoped that change would just take place?

Of course not! We now needed to work as a team to come up with an action plan. It was important that the team members took ownership of the actions. Therefore, I organized a session to generate an action plan. And what a difficult and insightful step that turned out to be. Let's move on to Step 5.

Step 6: Develop an Action Plan for Inclusion

I had categorized the problems into three kinds:

- *Straightforward:* Things that were straightforward where no discussion was needed and which just needed to be fixed. For example, one of the things the stories revealed was how often female employees were told by male employees, "I don't want a woman to tell me what to do."

- *Systemic:* Systemic barriers that management needed to address. For example, all government paperwork in that country was in the local language, and when foreigners came to the country to work, they needed assistance with managing that paperwork.

- *Discussion:* Things that needed discussion. For example, some stories revealed that, when English-speaking team members spoke in a meeting, they often spoke too fast. Telling them to slow down would certainly not be a solution. If it was that simple, they would have already done it. We needed to discuss what *fast* was.

I started the session with the first category, thinking it would just be a matter of explaining to people that they should not use statements like the example above about women. But when I asked for their acknowledgment of the issue, I got none. I was puzzled and baffled. I later learned that my attempt to make people publicly say that those who did this were wrong was not aligned to the local culture. Harmony is an important part of the local culture, and they will never say someone is wrong. I got through the rest of the session with a huge amount of support from the leader and made some progress, but with a question always niggling away inside my head. Does simply knowing where inclusion is not being practiced make people want to embrace DEI?

Let's elaborate on that niggling question.

At this stage of the project, we had figured out what was wrong but hadn't yet built the desire among the employees to embrace DEI. People understood the mistakes they were making but still didn't understand why they needed DEI. Remember, I had simply assumed that everyone would want to be inclusive, but the point was still not clear to them. And somehow the country's shrinking workforce didn't seem to be something that employees wanted to take responsibility for. Their opinion might be summarized thus: "It's the nation's and company's problem, not mine."

So, what next?

Step 7: Develop the Narrative

We had reached the stage where we needed to develop a narrative that the teams could take ownership of. If communication was the challenge, they had to own it and own not just the spoken words. We ran a week-long session where I worked with some 60 leaders in the organization. Armed with the knowledge we had collected in the stories, we started to fill in the blanks of the narrative. In the end, the stories I had collected proved to be very helpful.

We followed the steps highlighted in Chapter 17 and 18 on building a maximal narrative. The core of the narrative was developed in collaboration with the leaders, who then added their individual take on the narratives to make it relevant to their departments.

I won't share here all the steps we used to develop the narratives, as we have already done this earlier in the book, but I will share some key things we observed that helped lead to the ultimate success of the narrative:

- **The new identity:** The earlier proposition, "We should have diversity because we have a skills shortage," was replaced with a nudge to a new identity. The team came up with the following reason to have DEI:

  DEI helps us continue to prosper in our city and to bring our authentic selves to work. Bringing our authentic selves to work leads to innovation and success as a company. As a result, it helps us lead a better quality of life.

This was very relevant for team members, and here's why:

- o They all knew there was a risk of the factory closing if they didn't perform, and they couldn't perform without enough manpower. They all wanted to live in their city.
- o They understood that, if there was inclusion, they could bring their authentic selves to work, where they could express themselves freely and without fear of judgment.
- o When they had inclusion, they would have innovation and success as a company. Innovation would make things better and make sure everyone contributed to the success of the company. This would lead to them having a better quality of life and not working long hours. Innovation will make their processes efficient and save them time.

- **The leader's personal story:** This made one of the biggest differences to the narrative, as the leader had to think about a time in their life when they had had the experience of not being included and how this had made them feel. Excellent personal stories were shared which transformed not only the tellers, who were reminded of the difficulties they had once faced, but also the listeners, for whom the stories served as guides on how to be and do better. The process of finding these stories and being able to share them also built up rapport between leaders and team members. The vulnerability demonstrated in the stories became a bridge for connection. For the first time, we witnessed technical leaders become people's leaders.

- **Accountability and support:** Once the leader knew they had to build a 15- to 18-minute TED-style presentation of the narrative, they took ownership and felt accountable. We provided support and space for them to dig deep and ensure transformation took place.

These above mentioned factors catalyzed change.

As I write this chapter, I am running a similar DEI project in Riyadh, KSA and I am reminded of one of the most important aspects of this work, the role of the leader. If you do not have a visionary and courageous leader supporting you, you will never succeed with such a narrative. Not only have I been fortunate to have them, but the person leading this project is a deciding factor in whether we will take it on or not.

Let's take this chapter's pledge.

I pledge to remember and apply the following lessons:

- Diversity, equity, and inclusion (DEI) narratives are becoming ever more important in a diverse, globalized workforce.
- Diversity by itself is not enough to build an effective workforce; inclusion is vital, too.
- Before you develop your DEI narrative, source, analyze, and categorize your stories carefully: The lessons they reveal are not always what you expect!
- Make sure your DEI narratives are transformational and relevant.
- Narratives are most effective when accountability is given and support is provided.

So let's turn our attention to that successful DEI narrative.

CHAPTER 25

How to Decide When to Use Which Strategic Narrative

* * *

Estimated reading time: 6 minutes

> *The more you build narratives, the better your decisions become about when to use which narrative.*

As you hone your storytelling skills over time, you'll develop an ability to decide whether you want to use a maximal or a minimal narrative. But here are some guiding principles if you're a rookie.

For Employees, Maximal Narratives Work Better ...

- because it is insightful for employees who work *in* the business and not *on* the business
- because employees' knowledge about the pressure to change is often limited.

Their limited knowledge about why the organization they work for is changing is reflected in the way they respond to questions asked about the change. Let's go through some of the questions I have asked about change as well the answers employees have given.

In the first example, the change was automation in the factory line.

Question:"Why are you adopting automation?

Answer:"We have a lot more work, and it's not possible to do it manually."

Question:"Why are you making your factory smart?"

Answer:"That is the only way to sustain our presence."

In the next example, the change being introduced was hotdesking.

Question"Why are you hotdesking?"

Answer"The management introduced the policy to save space."

Such responses show little understanding of why change is actually taking place or why there is pressure to change at all. Let's continue asking employees questions, building on the answers we've received so far. In the first scenario:

Answer:"We have a lot more work, and it is not possible to do it manually."

My response:"OK, so, how have you managed to do it for years, and why is this suddenly an issue?"

Answer:"That is the only way to sustain our presence."

Question: "All right. I mean you have sustained your presence for so long, but how was that possible?"

And then there's no further response!

Every single time there comes a point beyond which employees have no clue why the change is needed. My suggestion then is to look further, look broader, and ask them what has changed in their world.

Questions to Get Employees to Understand the Pressure to Change

- Have there been any macroeconomic shifts such as hikes in interest rates or inflation?

- Has there been a change in competitive dynamics such as a new competitor or an old competitor modifying their strategies?

- Has there been a management change in terms of personnel or tactics?

- Has digital impacted this change?

Mostly, employees are unable to answer these questions. Industry insights are often not known to employees. As a result, maximal narratives highlighting these changes make these insights real and interesting for them.

Maximal Narratives Showcase a Clear and Bright Future

Maximal narratives focus on showing a very clear, bright future—an imagined success in which all employees want to take part and providing a motivating goal for people to pursue.

In one of our change storytelling projects, we shared a future story accompanied by a visual of employees on top of Singapore's iconic Marina Bay Sands building. It was incredible to watch employees' reactions when we shared the visual. They experienced themselves feeling the success because it had been so beautifully visualized.

Maximal narratives make your employees feel as though the organization has time for them. Leaders care enough to take them through why they need to change and how the leaders will bring the employees along on the journey. Maximal narratives take time to tell. And that's OK. Your audience wants you to invest time in them.

Indra Nooyi, ex-CEO of PepsiCo, mentioned this in an interview with John L. Weinberg at the University of Delaware. Communication, she says, is a much underestimated requirement in organizations. In the same interview, she shares that her sales meetings often run to almost two hours because she needs to show her willingness to give her time to her salespeople and make sure they are on her side. A quick 15-minute story just won't cut the mustard. This is quite a different approach from the commonly touted one which is to say only what is required and quickly! The time you give to the employees can be a way of demonstrating your care.

The clear difference between a boardroom full of senior leaders and a hall full of employees is that senior leaders want you to quickly share how you will solve a problem. Employees want you to give them time and show them how much you care.

Once you've learned how to build a maximal narrative, it's important to understand that the successful implementation of change using a maximal narrative is also dependent on how to cascade it down to the rank and file.

Cascading the Narrative

The process usually begins at the top. You work with the CEO of the organization and get the story ready. This story will need to address organizational needs but may not focus on specific departmental needs. For example, if you're telling a story about a system change that will make the procurement team more productive, why would the research and development team care?

The CEO's story is usually an *umbrella story* that needs to be made relevant for specific departments. When the department head tells the story, he or she needs to change the personal story at the beginning. Relevance is important if the story is to be sticky. If we don't look at departmental needs and streamline the story further, its nonspecific nature will distract the audience.

When Minimal Narratives Work Better

Minimal narratives are shorter because we start from the problems and don't really try to understand how they arose. Mostly, I use minimal narratives with senior business leaders because I don't need them to understand what macro trends are affecting us. They already know this. What I do is to make the problem we are trying to solve real by telling them a story, instead of a distillation of facts.

Another scenario in which I use minimal narratives is during the embryonic stages of change implementation—when I don't have a lot of detailed knowledge about the consequences of the change but I nonetheless want to create a positive feeling toward adopting the change. Minimal narratives are also good for a stage-like environment, where we are usually time bound.

In conclusion:

Maximal narratives work well for:

- employees
- when you have time.

Minimal narratives are for:

- managers
- at early stages of change
- on stage
- discussions in meetings
- corridor conversations
- when you are time poor.

This summary offers only a guideline. Sometimes I have used a maximal narrative for bosses and a minimal narrative for employees. The more you work on these narratives, the better your intuition becomes on which type of narrative to select.

You have almost learned everything about strategic storytelling now. However, there are some small things I have learned, either from my own experience or from books, that can enrich your storytelling. I call them "the little things that make strategic storytelling stronger"—*the tiny yet mighty practices*. I will share these with you in the next chapter, but first let's take this chapter's pledge.

I pledge to remember and apply the following lessons:

- For employees, maximal narratives usually works better because they are unaware of the need for change.
- For employees, a maximal narrative works better because the time invested in the narrative indicates they are cared for.
- Maximal narratives show employees succeeding in the future.
- Minimal narratives work better for time-poor environments, such as those of managers and leaders.
- For leaders, minimal narratives work better because they are focused on solutions, not on how we landed in the situation.

In the final chapter, you will find a collection of the tiny yet mighty practices that increase the probability of your success with storytelling.

CHAPTER 26

Making Strategic Storytelling Stronger

● ● ●

Estimated reading time: 13 minutes

The tiny yet mighty practices of storytelling.

For close to a decade now, I've been helping my clients steer their success using stories. Along the way, I have picked up many tiny yet mighty practices, either through experience or by reading books, that have helped my clients make their storytelling stronger and driven their success.

This chapter is a collection of those practices.

Practice 1: Dealing With the Super-Smart People While Implementing Organizational Change

Karen is responsible for change management in her organization. Every time she announces a change initiative, there is a group of people who hijack her presentations. They question everything and anything, which usually kills the little enthusiasm that exists for change. This group of people are the super-smart and hard-to-please types of the organization.

For a long time, before any change was announced, Karen's biggest worry was this group of people. After years of being grilled in presentations by them, Karen realized that, although super-smart people do question everything, the one thing they are driven by is the desire to be trailblazers. It's who they are. It's their identity. Let's not forget, the ability to question and achieve is what has made them super-smart.

So, what can we do with this insight? When announcing a change, start with a story of what achievements that change will make possible for the super-smart—describing, for example, world-changing innovations or transformational R&D, and how they as trailblazers will play a key role. Before you give them the playbook on how to change, tell them a story of achievement, and you'll then start hearing lines like "I love the challenge involved in this project!" Super-smart types are driven by a desire to be world class, and you can establish this opportunity from the onset. Think awards, patents, recognition … anything that throws a spotlight on them. If you have them in your audience, create an additional identity for them. Additional because they are at the edges and the identity that will excite most people will not excite them. They love a challenge, and as a storyteller we can leverage this.

Practice 2: The Words We Use in the Stories We Tell

Words are not just a mechanism of sharing information; they are a mechanism of influence. The following are three research-based findings from Robert Cialdini's book *Pre-Suasion: A Revolutionary Way to Influence and Persuade* that prove that words are a mechanism of influence.

1. USE WORDS CONNOTING ACHIEVEMENT

Research indicates that using the language of achievement (win, grow, succeed, master) improves performance and more than doubles their motivation. You can use this to your advantage in storytelling.

An important component of change narratives is telling a positive, upbeat story of the future when the change is implemented. Use words to connote achievement in the future story. When building a positive future story filled with words to connote achievement, one thing to be mindful of is to keep things realistic and subtle. You don't want to run the risk of sounding unrealistic since the future has not yet arrived. Keep the details minimal.

2. BROADEN THE SPECTRUM OF EMOTIONS

When you ask someone, "What's the problem?" they will look for a problem, even if there isn't one. This happens because, as humans, we tend to hunt for confirmation of statements rather than disconfirmation.

I use this insight when eliciting stories for change narratives. Rather than asking, "Tell me about a time when you were unhappy about a decision made in your organization?" I ask, "Tell me about a time when you were happy *or* unhappy about a decision made in your organization?" Cover both ends of the spectrum, happy and unhappy. Otherwise, you run the risk of finding only what you ask for, which may or may not be the complete truth.

3. AVOID VIOLENCE-LADEN WORDS

Violence-laden language is sometimes used in corporate settings on the grounds that it gives an adrenaline rush to people thereby making them perform better. However, when we are at work, we are not out on the battlefield. Replace violence-laden language with achievement-laden language. Avoid words like "target" or "beat" and instead use words like "desired identity" and "trailblaze."

In addition, my experience has taught me one more thing about the use of words when inspiring change in organizations with storytelling ...

4. DON'T USE THE WORD CHANGE

This may sound crazy, but sometimes just using the word *change* can derail change implementation. Why? Because even just the word *change* can make us feel weary. We have heard it, experienced it, and struggled with it, and we don't like it. There are many other words and phrases such as *a new future*, *a better future*, and so on, that we can use to replace the word *change*. When we say the word *change* it feels as though we have to endure a shift from one state to another, but *new future* is inviting, a place we want to go to. I don't feel any baggage with the term *new future* but I do feel it with *change*.

Practice 3: Never Incentivize the Change Behavior

In 2017, I was invited to speak on storytelling for change at a learning festival of an organization. I was surprised to notice that the employees attending my talk were given a stamp on their "learning passports": Once they had a certain number of stamps, they could win prizes such as iPads and other consumer desirables. This incentivized learning puzzled me.

Coincidentally, that same day, Susanna Gallani published an article in the *Harvard Business Review* entitled "Incentives Don't Help People Change, but Peer Pressure Does." The article gives great insights into why peer pressure is a better strategy than incentives for change. Gallani shares a study from a California hospital whose data showed the contrasting effects of incentives and peer pressure on hand hygiene practices.

The hospital ran a hand hygiene campaign among its employees for 90 days. If you practiced good hand hygiene, you could get a bonus of $1,200. Physicians were not eligible to participate in this campaign, as under Californian law physicians cannot be hospital employees, as opposed to, say, nurses or technicians. During the campaign, employees who were eligible for the bonus improved their hand hygiene, but after it ended, hand hygiene dropped to the same level or worse than before. The physicians, on the other hand, were slow to improve but maintained high levels of hand hygiene performance over the remainder of the period.

The physicians did not qualify for the bonus, so the staff found alternative ways to encourage them to improve their hand hygiene practices. These methods were not monetary incentives, but examples included creating hand-shaped paper cards with the names of doctors who demonstrated good hand hygiene practices, and sending celebratory emails or respectful reminders from the chief nursing officer.

In summary, the monetary incentives led to a more significant improvement, but it was only temporary. In contrast, the peer-pressure techniques resulted in a lasting change in organizational behaviour even after the incentive period ended.

You can use this insight in your storytelling by:

- not incentivizing the change in behavior
- giving recognition to those who practice change with storytelling publicly, for example by sharing their success stories.

Practice 4: Don't Apologize for the Change or Emphasize Its Difficulties

The delivery of most change messages starts with something like this:

- "*I am sorry* we are changing the way we do ticketing."
- "*I am sorry* we are having to put you through yet another change."
- "The new change will *come with difficulties.*"

Unknowingly, we sound apologetic about the change or focus on all the difficulties associated with the change. As a result, we fail to show the bright side of the change. Change implementation is difficult, no doubt, but the actual change is beneficial.

For example, if the change you are announcing is:

We are adding a new hospital to an already existing hospital cluster, and as a part of the cluster now the new hospital will share resource with us.

rather than saying,

I am really sorry, but we have to help them, and I am aware how hard this can be when we have so much on our plate already.

instead, tell a story where two hospitals working together caused something great to happen:

We have an amazing innovation that is going to take over the manual work of transporting the specimen bottles by hand. There is a technology we are adopting to transport the specimen bottle using a machine. This will also help with the manpower crunch we are facing, and we will have more time to do high-value work. We learned about how to make this change happen from hospital XYZ which just joined our cluster last month. Contrary to our original belief, they saved us time rather than taking our time.

Practice 5: To Turn a Disjointed Presentation Into a Story, Use Segue Lines

"Anjali, I am presenting to my team next week, can I go through the presentation with you?" a client asks. Next thing, we are on a Zoom call going through her presentation. Here's how she takes me through the sleek PowerPoint her corporate communications team has put together:

I will start by telling them what I will cover in the presentation. Then, I will share the results from last year on slides 2 and 3, and some opportunities we have for this year on slides 4 and 5. Slides 6 through 8 will cover some of the initiatives to fulfill those opportunities. And finally, the last two slides are dedicated to covering what the future looks like.

Most of us will call this a logical approach. And that's exactly where the problem lies. The way we get ready for presentations has been ineffective for so long that the wrong has become the norm.

Knowing what to say on a slide is like knowing about *one* event in a story only. But a story is not just about singular events. As we know from Chapter 10, it is a series of *connected* events.

In Figure 26.1, you can see how each slide is an event, but for them to sound like a story they need to be connected with segue lines. In the absence of such connections, the slides become a disconnected series of events. All too often, you see presenters presenting like this:

Step 1: They click and the next slide appears.

Step 2: They see what's on the next slide.

Step 3: They talk about what they see on the slide …

and so on.

What makes a great presentation is when you:

Step 1: Present a slide.

Step 2: Build anticipation for the next slide.

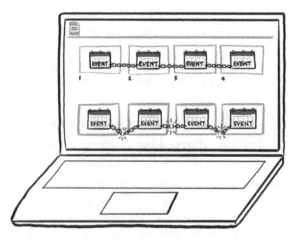

Figure 26.1 A story is a series of connected events

Step 3: Reveal the next slide.

Step 4: Talk about the next slide.

This problem largely occurs because our preparation for a presentation generally ends at content development. It rarely goes on to connecting the content developed on each slide. Since we have put no attention and thought into creating a connection between slides, we have no choice but to see what is on the next slide before we can talk about it. The natural progression and flow of words to connect the slides is stripped away.

Segue, or transition, lines should connect the slides when we listen to a presenter. We feel as though we are hearing a story, and this results in high levels of engagement.

The choice of segue line is dependent on the context and content. Here are a couple of examples based on context:

	Context	Segue line	Content
1	Before I share results for the year	*So, how did we do this year?*	Click now, slide comes on, and then present
2	Before I share opportunities for the year	*So, what is your opportunity for the year?*	Click now, slide comes on, and then present

You will notice there is a pattern in the above examples: I ask the question as a segue line and then the content of my slide becomes the answer to the question.

Think of the content of the next slide you are presenting, then ask a question to which your next slide becomes the answer.

To illustrate one of my golden rules to create great segues, here is a list of some commonly used segue lines:

- "Let me share what I mean."
- "Let me give you an example."
- "What exactly does this mean?"
- "Some of you may be thinking ..."

If you practice using segue lines, your presentations will quickly sound more like a story. A question you must learn to ask yourself is: "And before I move on to the next slide, what should I say?"

Gail Anderson from Applause Inc. has written a fantastic blog on segue lines. Here I list some of the most important points she makes. The examples given are mine, but the segue idea is Gail Anderson's.

- Sometimes you can simply say: "The next slide shows us the growth we have seen in various regions in the last quarter." It's a simple transition from one slide to the next.

- Use the header of your slide to create a perfect segue. Say, for example, the header is "Top Three Actions," you can say, " We have just learned about our growth strategy, and to bring that strategy to life we will start with the following Top Three Actions." What you see written on the slide is only "Top Three Actions" but you have verbalized the segue line.

- When you are done presenting a slide, anchor the content of the slide with a summarizing statement. For example, "So, all the points I mentioned in this slide will help us achieve the growth we are looking at, but what exactly is this growth?" Notice how you have summarized the points of the slide and also set yourself up for a seamless transition to the next slide.

Segues are what makes a disjointed PowerPoint presentation a series of events—a story.

We have now come to the end of this chapter, and you know the drill: It's time to take a pledge.

I pledge to remember and apply the following lessons:

- Build a trailblazer identity for super-smart people when implementing change in an organization.
- Use words connoting achievement.
- Avoid violence-laden words.
- Don't use the word *change* when announcing change in an organization.
- Never incentivize change behavior.
- Don't apologize for introducing change into an organization.
- Use segue lines to turn a disjointed PowerPoint into a succinct series of events.

Believe it or not, it is time to conclude this book. But before I do so, I want to remind you that while this book may have come to an end, your journey to success with storytelling has only just begun ... What matters is not so much what you have learned from this book, but how you apply what you have learned to drive your success.

Conclusion

You've just finished reading this book, and your head is swimming with ideas. You're probably wondering, "Where do I begin?"

Well, let's start with the summary:

In Part I, we learned how adopting the identity of a marketer teaches us the importance of connection, which is fundamental to strategic storytelling.

In Part II, we learned that strategic storytelling is not reserved for leaders in organizations (a common myth). If you reflect and focus on finding stories, and then adopt the identity of a reporter to tell those stories effectively, you are a strategic storyteller from the day you start work in the organization.

In Part III, you learned about the fourth identity: a visionary storyteller – someone who helps people see the future and, more importantly, see their own success in the future. The tool the visionary uses to do this and make change happen is a strategic corporate narrative.

As a storytelling practitioner I have read many books on storytelling, but out of all the books I have read, there are two I love the most and have learned the most from. They are *All Marketers Tell Stories* by Seth Godin and *The Leader's Guide to Storytelling* by Stephen Denning.

The interesting thing about these two books is they are opposite in many ways. Seth's book makes a compelling case to understand your audience's worldview and then tell a story to fit their worldview. Denning's book teaches you how to make your message stick in a corporate world using stories.

Simply put, take a storyline with the components of Audience, Message, and Story. Seth's writing teaches you to start at Audience whereas Denning's teaches you to start from Message.

As I read these books and gained my experience in storytelling, it became clear to me the learnings from Seth's book can do wonders in the consumer world, but a lot of the learnings were hard to apply in a corporate boardroom. There was a focus on empathy, emotions, worldview, human desires, and feelings.

And if you have worked in a corporate setting, you will know that we stay away from these things in that world. A corporate boardroom conversation is often filled with shareholder returns, goals, targets, revenue, productivity, and profit. A human-centric story often fails in this environment. When you do try to tell it, you are shot down and asked to get to the point.

I fell in love with Seth's work and practiced human-centric stories in a boardroom and fell on my face. I found application, connection, and meaning for Seth's work in the consumer space, on stage, in commercials, but failed to apply the learnings in the boardroom.

On the other hand, Denning's writing was a brilliant guide for the boardroom, filled with practical, logical, and methodical ways to make your messages stick in a boardroom. It made the bosses and stakeholders happy. But every now and then, I felt this doesn't connect with me at a human level.

It is great for a strategy rollout, but if I was an employee who needed to be a part of the strategy rollout, what would be in it for me? What I noticed was that I could get boardroom success out of the practical application of Denning's storytelling teachings, but I wasn't sure I was making change happen on the ground.

It almost felt like a fight between my head and heart. It became clear to me that in a business-to-consumer world, consumers pay, so we do everything to tug to their heartstrings and do empathy-filled storytelling. But in a corporate world, employees do not directly generate revenue, so we do not tell stories designed for them.

As a human I leaned toward Seth's work and as a corporate professional I leaned toward Denning's. Because most of my work is corporate, as a professional, I would refer to Denning's work. But at the end of the day, I would question myself and say, "Really? Is boardroom success all you are after, or are you interested in making change happen on the ground?"

I wanted to apply the principles of Seth's writing in a corporate boardroom, but I knew I would only be successful if I stuck to Denning's teachings. But truth be told, it didn't feel good. And this constant nudging led me to unconsciously start sliding Seth's work into the boardroom drip by drip (I have learned to say drip by drip from Seth which means slowly. Slowly like an IV puts medicine in your veins.)

This is what started to happen:

When a company head would say, "We are running this change initiative to be a model site for diversity, equity and inclusion, I would say, "Why should your people care? Surely you need them to make this happen?"

When a company head would say, "We are bringing in automation, robotics, and artificial intelligence to increase productivity." I would say, "And why should your people care? Are they going to benefit from productivity?"

I started to treat the employees like consumers.

I began asking this question because Seth's writing had taught me about empathy. I was putting myself in an employee's shoes and it was the question coming to my head—why should I care?

I wasn't sure if I was going to be successful by asking these questions, but I still did it. I started with empathy, worldviews, human desires. When I knew what people wanted to hear, I would structure the story like Denning taught in his writing.

Seth's work helped me mine the right story and Denning's work helped me tell the right story, and project after project, success started to roll in.

What I learned was I could find a perfect story blend to be practical, logical, methodical, emotional, empathy filled even in the driest corporate scenarios.

When you seek to make a change happen in your organizations, you must treat your teams like the most important people. Because you need them the most to make the change happen.

I am often perplexed why Human Resources departments have been trying to solve the same problem for years now—how to motivate people? The reason might be because we don't tell stories to fit with their worldview. Granted they don't swipe their credit cards to help us achieve our targets or make us look good in front of the shareholders or our HQ. But they make the products, services, and offerings that move our balance sheets.

Strategic Storytelling is an invitation to drive your success with stories.

Congratulations, you are now fully equipped to be a Strategic Storyteller, one who knows why some stories drive success at work but others don't.

You can now go make the change happen with stories and drive your success.

211

Appendix: Your Complete Storytelling Pledge

Chapter 1

- If the goal of my communication is to make a connection, then storytelling is my best tool to do it.
- My communication cannot just be *correct*; it also has to *connect*.
- I must never assume I know my audiences well. I must try to understand their emotions, create resonance, build connection, and then drive the desired action. That's what a true marketer storyteller does.
- Storytelling is not about solving the problem per se but solving the negative emotion associated with the problem.

Chapter 2

- Vulnerability is a strong bridge of connection between people. It is permission to be imperfect.
- If a well-told factual story is like glue, a story that resonates is like superglue.
- If your goal is to shift knowledge into understanding for those who can't have the same experiences as you, tell a story. Stories are experience simulators.
- Big stories are great attention grabbers but weak catalysts for creating a change through the inspiration generated in the story. Small stories have a higher probability of making a change happen. A story is big or small depending on the degree of the unexpected events in the story.
- A core story needs to have many strategic stories drawn out of it to make a connection with different kinds of audience.

- We all have a story bias. We only have a certain audience in our mind who we want to tell the story to. If the story works for that audience, we tend to believe it works for everyone. We just don't see the other audiences. They remain invisible to us. Therefore, before you begin building a story, be very clear on who the story is for.

Chapter 3

- You can only create a connection when you understand the context of the connection.
- The context of connection is about understanding the who, why, and how of the connection.
- There are stories to inspire and stories to influence.
- Influence is the capacity to change thinking; inspiration is the capacity to fire action.
- Because there are a lot more negative emotions associated with the decisions we make in the boardroom, we must use influence to shape decisions in the boardroom. Inspiration is more emotion-based, while influence is more thinking-based.
- Influencing our audience is a better strategy for a boardroom because the decisions we make affect a lot more people. Our responsibility is so much greater.

Chapter 4

- Depending on who you are telling a story to in a corporate environment, you will need to make your story either maximal or minimal. A maximal story is one that is well developed, while minimal means it is spare (less detailed) in nature.
- Minimal stories are concise and task oriented and focus on the point more than the characters in the story.
- For leaders, the stories that show organizational success are important because that is the role they have in the organization. They are directly responsible for making sure the organization succeeds. Therefore, stories that focus on TIM (time, image, and money) work well for leadership. They succeed when they can show the organization is succeeding.

- For employees, you must show their success. For example, if you tell an employee to do something because it leads to the organization becoming efficient, the employee will not be as enthused; however, if you ask the employee to do something that makes them efficient and as a result gives them the time to be part of a team that is leading innovation in the organization, then their enthusiasm will shine through. Their success leads to organizational success, but you need to find their success in the success of the organization.

Chapter 5

- Understanding the storytelling vocabulary helps us build better strategic stories.
- Empathy is the key and the starting point of strategic storytelling.
- A worldview is a collection of attitudes, values, stories, and expectations about the world around us, informing our every thought and action.
- When something resonates it is because we have said something that reminds someone of something. We know we have built resonance when we elicit responses from people.
- Connection is the energy existing between people when they feel seen, heard, and valued.
- Strategic storytelling takes place when we *empathize* with our audience. As a result, we understand their *worldviews*, which enables us to build *resonance* using our storytelling. And resonance creates *connection* and moves people into action.

Chapter 6

- The visionary leader is not the only storyteller identity.
- A strategic corporate storyteller has multiple storytelling identities they can adopt: a reflective, journalist, reporter, and marketer storyteller.
- A reflective storyteller reflects on their own experiences and observes the experiences of those around them to find a moment and use that moment to make a point.
- A journalist storyteller finds stories by reading, researching, surfing the net, and conducting story-mining exercises.

- In the process of finding and telling a story, you don't just adopt one identity but many identities along the way.

Chapter 7

- I don't have to look for stories with big, unexpected events to be a changemaker.
- Stories with small unexpected events have the power to make me a successful changemaker.

Chapter 8

- Becoming a reporter means you can tell your story in a compelling way.
- There are two types of stories every corporate should learn to tell: maximal and minimal.
- Maximal stories are rich in detail and acknowledge that the audience wants to listen to the full story so that it resonates with them.
- There are four key steps to telling a story:
  - Step 1 is about being a marketer storyteller and structuring the key message in such a way that it connects.
  - Step 2 is about being a reflective and journalist storyteller and finding the story you can tell.
  - Step 3 is again about being a marketer storyteller and ensuring the story resonates.
  - Step 4 is about assembling the story.

Chapter 9 and 10

- The maximal story has seven elements:
  - Using time markers, calendar markers, and place markers helps you position yourself as someone who is telling the truth, much like a reporter.
  - Activating visualization is a good strategy because we think and feel in images. Leveraging schemas is a good way to activate visualization.
  - Stories have people, and people have names.
  - Bringing in emotion, by describing (not displaying) emotions.
  - Using connected series of events to bring connection.

- Using the unexpected to make the story insightful.
- Reiterating the key message at the end of the story, as this is what matters most to the corporate audience—the focus here should be on the action part of the key message.

Chapter 11

- For management, we should make our stories minimal.
- The reason for minimal storytelling is not just time, but because management's connection points are different from those of other employees.
- Some of the tactics you can use to make your story minimal are:
  - Don't use the word *story*.
  - Don't develop your characters too much.
  - Make the story invisible.
  - Build the story proposition around TIM—time, image, money.
  - Reduce the number of events.

Chapter 12

- The story proposition is as important as the point or the key message of the story.
- The point is often a succinct, to-the-point line, while the proposition is the idea behind that point.
- The story proposition should not be built around the most obvious point you see in the story.
- If you are telling a strategic story, then your proposition should take up 50 percent of the telling time. It's as important as the story.

Chapter 13

- It is not just the leadership team who can and should tell stories.
- Story brand ambassadors help tell the story in informal environments where the corporate culture lives.
- For a change you anticipate will face resistance, it helps to have two-pronged approach, with both leaders and story brand ambassadors telling the story.

Chapter 14

- Stories are lessons from the past; narratives are forward-looking.
- Stories almost always have a character; narratives may or may not have a character.
- A story can be part of a narrative.
- Generally speaking, narrative unfolds over a longer timeframe.
- Stories make a point; narratives ask people to adopt new ways of doing things.

Chapter 15

- Stories are a good solution for helping us understand something better.
- Narratives are a good solution for taking us toward a future we want to be a part of.
- Stories make a point, but narratives show me the path ahead.
- Situations where we should tell a story include:
  - responding to specific questions
  - when we are in a time-poor situation and when a story will suffice
  - in informal and conversational environments.
- Situations where we should share a narrative include:
  - launching a change in an organization
  - a new product rollout.
  - a new strategy rollout.
  - a new campaign rollout
  - when asking for funds or resources for a new initiative
  - simply answering why we are doing what we are doing.

Chapter 17

- A leader's goal is not to get agreement but to get alignment.
- Agreement without action is useless.
- For too long we have relied on clear, concise, and credible reasons and messages to make change happen. This, however, is not a sound strategy.
- Today, the role of a leader is to be a visionary because knowledge is democratized and the speed of change is the only certainty.

Chapter 18

- A change proposition is often meaningless to employees because it focuses entirely on business profitability.

- An opportunity to share a strategic corporate narrative is often missed because we fail to see an opportunity due to our entrenched ways of communicating in a corporate setting.

- A successful change is not a result of careful analysis of the problem, then finding a solution and then asking people to change. It is a result of making people see something, feel something, and then giving them the fire in their belly to want to change.

- People accept changes they're emotionally invested in.

Chapter 19, 20, and 21

- Maximal narrative steps are
    - Step 1: Provide your listeners with a new identity.
    - Step 2: Engage your audience with a leader's personal story.
    - Step 3: Connect the leader's personal change to the organizational change.
    - Step 4: Get your audience to see the need to change.
    - Step 5: Provide a story of someone negatively impacted by the problem.
    - Step 6: Add data to establish the magnitude of the problem.
    - Step 7: Put in place change assistance.
    - Step 8: Show how your change assistance will help the individual.
    - Step 9: Show what the future holds.
    - Step 10: Address premade stories.

Chapter 22

- There are four steps to the minimal change narrative:
    - Step 1: Nudge your audience toward a new identity, or state the point to motivate change
    - Step 2: Share a story of a person who has been negatively impacted.
    - Step 3: Share a success/positive story.
    - Step 4: Invite your audience to make their own mind up on what is the future they see for themselves.

Chapter 23

- Digital transformation narratives are one of the most needed narratives in corporate organizations today.
- Employees in organizations have not yet become comfortable with digital transformation and feel threatened by it. The fear lies in the belief they may be replaced by a robot or automation.
- It is the leader's role to shape and tell narratives to infuse the desire in people to want to change.
- Making the digital transformation narrative relevant so it resonates is key.

Chapter 24

- Diversity, equity, and inclusion (DEI) narratives are becoming ever more important in a diverse, globalized workforce.
- Diversity by itself is not enough to build an effective workforce; inclusion is vital, too.
- Before you develop your DEI narrative, source, analyze, and categorize your stories carefully: The lessons they reveal are not always what you expect!
- Make sure your DEI narratives are transformational and relevant.
- Narratives are most effective when accountability is given and support is provided.

Chapter 25

- For employees, maximal narratives usually work better because they are unaware of the need for change.
- For employees, a maximal narrative works better because the time invested in the narrative indicates they are cared for.
- Maximal narratives show employees succeeding in the future.
- Minimal narratives work better for time-poor environments, such as those of managers and leaders.
- For leaders, minimal narratives work better because they are focused on solutions, not on how we landed in the situation.

Chapter 26

- Build a trailblazer identity for super-smart people when implementing change in an organization.
- Use words connoting achievement.
- Avoid violence-laden words.
- Don't use the word *change* when announcing change in an organization.
- Never incentivize change behavior.
- Don't apologize for introducing change into an organization.
- Use segue lines to turn a disjointed PowerPoint into a succinct series of events.

References

Preface

Oshiro, J. (2022, February 26) as told to Anjali Sharma, Narrative The Business of Stories. Storytelling: Is "Safety First" the most crucial aspect in running a business? YouTube. https://www.youtube.com/watch?v=8SORk7SNMjo

Introduction

Godin, S. (2019). *This is marketing: You can't be seen until you learn to see.* Penguin Business.

Switzer, K. (2009). *Marathon Woman: Running the Race to Revolutionize Women's Sports.* Da Capo Press.

Chapter 2

Grant, A. (2014). *Give and Take: Why Helping Others Drives Our Success.* Penguin

Chapter 3

Brown, B. (2009). *Daring Greatly: How the Courage to Be Vulnerable Transforms the Way We Live, Love, Parent and Lead.* Portfolio Penguin.

Chapter 5

Brown, B. (2010). *The Gifts of Imperfection: Let Go of Who You Think You're Supposed to Be and Embrace Who You Are.* Hazelden.

Nadella, S. (2019). *HIT REFRESH: The Quest to Rediscover Microsoft's Soul and Imagine Better Future for Everyone*. Harper Business.

Chapter 6

Denning, S. (2007). *The Secret Language of Leadership: How Leaders Inspire Action through Narrative*. John Wiley & Sons.
Hessan, D. (2014, April 10). *To get to know your customers, spend a day in their underwear*. Inc. https://www.inc.com/diane-hessan/to-get-to-know-your-customers-spend-a-day-in-their-underwear.html
Sharma, A. (2021, October 15). *Why Data without Empathy is Empty*. Forbes. ForbesBusinessCouncil.www.forbes.com/sites/forbesbusinesscouncil/2021/10/15/why-data-without-empathy-is-empty/?sh=23e85d7263f4

Chapter 7

Eilperin, J. (2016, September 13). *White House Women Want to be in the Room Where It Happens*. The Washington Post. www.washingtonpost.com/news/powerpost/wp/2016/09/13/white-house-women-are-now-in-the-room-where-it-happens/

Chapter 8

Lumia, N. (2022). *You're a Story Teller*. [Video]. Vimeo. https://vimeo.com/204577767?embedded=true&source=video_title&owner=1379004
Miller, D. (2017). *Building a Story Brand: Clarify Your Message So Customers Will Listen*. Thomas Nelson Publishers.
Walk That Bass. (2017, April 19). *3. What is the difference between a noise and a note?*. [Video]. YouTube. www.youtube.com/watch?v=bCm6VpCE9Qc
Phone Trailers. (n.d.). You're a Storyteller: The Nokia Lumia 1520. [Video]. YouTube. https://www.youtube.com/watch?v=q2utZdGp450

Chapter 9

Callahan, S. (2016). *Putting Stories to Work: Mastering Business Storytelling*. Pepperberg Press.
Denning, S. (2010). *The Leader's Guide to Storytelling*. Jossey-Bass.

Medina, J. (2012, October 27). *Rule #10 Vision trumps all other senses.* Brain rules. https://brainrules.net/vision

Small, D. (2007, June 27). *To Increase Charitable Donations, Appeal to the Heart—Not the Head.* Knowledge at Wharton. https://knowledge.wharton.upenn.edu/article/to-increase-charitable-donations-appeal-to-the-heart-not-the-head/

Chapter 10

SteveJobsArchive. (2017, September 21). *Steve Jobs introduces iCloud & iOS 5 WWDC 2011.* [Video]. Youtube. www.youtube.com/watch?v=if4xq27l5Yk

Hansen, K. (2009). *Tell Me about Yourself: Storytelling to Get Jobs and Propel Your Career* JIST Works.

Hutchens, D. (2015). *Circle of the 9 Muses: A Storytelling Field Guide for Innovators and Meaning Makers.* Wiley.

Chapter 12

Gladwell, M. (2005). *Blink: The Power of Thinking without Thinking.* Little, Brown and Co.

Gallo, C. (2018). *Five Stars: The Communication Secrets to Get from Good to Great.* St. Martin's Press.

Chapter 13

Cialdini, R. (2016). *Pre-Suasion: A Revolutionary Way to Influence and Persuade.* Simon & Schuster.

Chapter 14

Nikiforova, B. (2012). http://repozytorium.uwb.edu.pl/jspui/handle/11320/345. Pogranicze. Studia Społeczne, 19, 7–20. https://doi.org/10.15290/pss.2012.19.01

Anjali Sharma, Narrative: The Business of Stories (2017, March 4) *Change Storytelling by Indra Nooyi.* [Video]. Youtube. https://www.youtube.com/watch?v=DsABAnILwj0&list=PLdi8fncW2wNMCuIUfudPDz0xEX-voKo476&index=7

Chapter 17

Calne, D.B. (2000). *Within Reason: Rationality and Human Behavior.* Vintage.

Friedman, T. L. (2017). *Thank You for Being Late: An Optimist's Guide to Thriving in the Age of Accelerations.* Picador Paper.

Anjali Sharma, Narrative: The Business of Stories (2017, March 4) *Change Storytelling by Indra Nooyi.* [Video]. Youtube. https://www.youtube.com/watch?v=DsABAnILwj0&list=PLdi8fncW2wNMCuIUfudPDz0xEX-voKo476&index=7

Chapter 18

Dr. John Kotter (2012, March 23). *The Heart of Change.* [Video]. YouTube. www.youtube.com/watch?v=1NKti9MyAAw

Chapter 19

Clear, J. (2019). *Atomic Habits: An Easy and Proven Way to Build Good Habits and Break Bad Ones.* Penguin Random House.

Heath, C & Heath, D. (2007). *Made to Stick: Why Some Ideas Survive and Others Die.* Random House.

Adam Morgan and Mark Barden (2015). *A Beautiful Constraint: How to Transform Your Limitations into Advantages, and Why It's Everyone's Business.* Hoboken, NJ: Wiley.

Singapore Airlines (2012, September 10). *Across the World with the Singapore Girl.* [Video]. Youtube. www.youtube.com/watch?v=mIkNzhM2b70

Chapter 20

Cialdini, R. (2016). *Pre-Suasion: A Revolutionary Way to Influence and Persuade.* Simon & Schuster.

Sandberg, S. (2010). *Why We Have Too Few Women Leaders.* TED Talk. www.ted.com/talks/sheryl_sandberg_why_we_have_too_few_women_leaders/transcript?language=en

Taylor, J. B. (2009). *My Stroke of Insight.* New American Library.

Chapter 22

Duarte, N. *How to Move Your Presentation Audience with This Powerful Story Technique.* www.duarte.com/presentation-skills-resources/move-presentation-audience-with-story-techniques-in-presentations/

Japhet G. & Feek, W. (2018, June 27). *Storytelling Can be a Force for Social Change. Here's How.* Media, Entertainment and Information, World Economic Forum. www.weforum.org/agenda/2018/06/storytelling-for-social-change-communication-initiative/.

King, S. (2010). Josie's Story: A Mother's Inspiring Crusade to Make Medical Care Safe. Grove Press. Also (2019). *The Josie King Story.* [Video]. Facebook. www.facebook.com/danlesterdabonhcs/videos/the-josie-king-story/2498078587080969/

Chapter 23

Newport, C. (2022). *Deep Work: Rules for Focused Success in a Distracted World.* Piatkus Books.

Chapter 25

University of Delaware (2019, April 15). *John L. Weinberg Distinguished Speaker: Indra Nooyi speaks at UD.* [Video]. YouTube. www.youtube.com/watch?v=h9NhVTLcqMo

Chapter 26

Cialdini, R. (2016) *Pre-Suasion: A Revolutionary Way to Influence and Persuade.* Simon & Schuster.

Gallani, S. (2017 March 23). *Incentives Don't Help People Change, But Peer Pressure Does. Harvard Business Review.* https://hbr.org/2017/03/incentives-dont-help-people-change-but-peer-pressure-does

Zack, G. C. (2017, October 20). *Your Questions: How Do You Create Segues in a Presentation without Spending Countless Hours Planning Them?.* Applause. www.applauseinc.net/blog-content/2017/10/20/your-questions-how-do-you-create-segues-in-a-presentation-without-spending-countless-hours-planning-them

Reflection pages

If you could teach 5 things you learnt from Strategic Storytelling what would they be? Please take a photo of your 5 key learnings and post it on your social channels. Tag us for a feature on our social channels! (Instagram @anjalistories or Anjali Sharma – Strategic Storytelling on LinkedIn)

Connect with the author

Website
www.narrative.com.sg

LinkedIn
https://www.linkedin.com/in/anjali-sharma-4973a642/

Instagram
https://www.instagram.com/anjalistories/

Would you like your people to read this book?

If you would like to discuss how you could bring these ideas to your team, we would love to hear from you. Our titles are available at competitive discounts when purchased in bulk across both physical and digital formats. We can offer bespoke editions featuring corporate logos, customized covers, or letters from company directors in the front matter can also be created in line with your special requirements.

We work closely with leading experts and organizations to bring forward-thinking ideas to a global audience. Our books are designed to help you be more successful in work and life.

For further information, or to request a catalogue, please contact:
business@johnmurrays.co.uk
sales-US@nicholasbrealey.com (North America only)

Nicholas Brealey Publishing is an imprint of
John Murray Press.